Our Journey of Love

5 Steps to Navigate Your Caregiving Journey

Susan J. Ryan

Dedication

This book is dedicated to my Daddy, Harold Francis Armstrong, and my husband, John Michael Ryan, the two men I cherish and adore, whose life journeys include their diagnoses of types of Dementia. Your journeys inspire me to become my very best and challenge me to support creating the best experiences for everyone I possibly can.

Thank you, God, for allowing my life to be
blessed by two such incredible men.

My Daddy, Harold Francis (Hal) Armstrong

My Husband, John Michael (Jack) Ryan

Epigraph

One of the greatest gifts of my journey in caregiving is learning to love myself and care intentionally for myself, as I love and intentionally care for those for whom I provide care. When I become my greatest, I have the capacity to both give my very best and experience the very best of our journey together.

Acknowledgements

There isn't enough room in one book to acknowledge everyone who has participated so valuably in my journey that led to the creation of *Our Journey of Love, 5 Steps to Navigate Your Caregiving Journey.* You are the countless guides who have taught and supported me over the years through my journeys of love. While I don't remember all your names, I do remember what you taught me and how you made me feel. Thank you.

I acknowledge those of you for whom I have provided support in types of care over these past thirty years. Out of respect for your privacy, I won't mention your names; I know you know how incredibly grateful I am for the opportunity to be part of your life. I am a better person for knowing and learning from you.

Daddy, you modeled kindness, love, respect, and hard work, throughout my life. One of the greatest gifts of love you gave me was continuously challenging me to think. I remember so many times coming to you with a question and, instead of you giving me an answer, you patiently taught me how to answer it myself, explaining to me how you wanted me to know how to think things through when you weren't there. Many of my lessons have new meanings now. You taught me then and you're still teaching me today. When a type of Dementia touched your mind, it didn't touch your spirit, your kindness, or your love. I love you Daddy.

My beloved husband Jack, I used to wonder why I hadn't met the man of my dreams. On our second date, I knew why. God didn't want me to miss the opportunity to share, and to cherish, each second of our time together. Thank you for loving me perfectly. Thank you for modeling the beauty of loving God purely. Thank you for creating an amazing spiritual journey of learning for us; it continues to teach me who I am. Jack, you are the love of my life and the man of my dreams. As we journey together with your diagnosis of Alzheimer's, you continue to love me perfectly, to teach me about loving God purely, and to prove how incredible the gifts of massive acceptance and radical presence are in our lives.

Janet Joy Hemphill Armstrong, my mother. I love you very much. I know how much you loved me and I am grateful to you for all you have taught me. So much of what I have learned about how much you loved me has come through repackaged lessons I continue to learn after your passing. I wish I had known how to love and support you better during your life; I love and honor you now in the ways I know mean the most to you. Thank you.

Donna Vollono Armstrong, my mother in love. Thank you for loving my Daddy so purely every second of your lives together. You taught me how to love, you taught me how to be a better care giver, and you continue to support me in my journey of love with Jack. I love you and I am incredibly grateful for you in my life.

Joe Ryan and Maureen Zakrzewski. Your continuous love and support of me as I love and care for your brother, Jack, mean so very much to me. Thank you for always being there for both of us.

Jack's sons Sean, Craig, Daniel and Patrick, and your amazing families. I came into your lives after your mom passed away. You accepted me then and you have continued to support me unconditionally in my care for your Dad. I love you all very much; I am so grateful to be in your lives. You are my family and I know I am truly blessed because of this.

Cynthia Davis, I have written and rewritten my words of gratitude for you. None of them touch its depth. Thank you for your wisdom, spirit, kindness, and guidance. Thank you for seeing in me that which I didn't know was there, guiding me to become who I didn't know I could be, and challenging me while supporting me; I'm excited about where you are guiding my journey. As I have been creating this book, you've been with me every word and every step of the way. This book would not be what it is without the words you shared just before I began writing; "Let your heart write your book." It did. Throughout this entire process you have been creating with me, questioning me, encouraging me, challenging me. When you agreed to write the foreword for my book, I was filled with gratitude. When I read what you created, I was moved to tears. You captured *Our Journey of Love* perfectly. I felt the emotions of the journey through your words and the importance of the oneness of our journey as care givers and care receivers. Your love and guidance strengthens my passion and purpose to positively touch people's lives on their journeys of love.

Lynn Pooley Hadjis, we have been traveling our journeys together since we were fourteen. I love you so very much. When I am in a low spot, the phone rings and you are there, or a card from you arrives in the mail with the perfect message. How often we used to laugh in surprise when this happened to one or the other of us; not anymore. I'm so glad we share this special connection. We share so many pieces of fabric in the quilts of our lives. When we have experienced what we cannot get our arms around, we are another pair of arms for each other. When we are so filled with joy we can't contain it, we pour into each other. You and your family surround me with love, believe in me, and are always there for me.

My treasured family and friends who I cannot imagine my life without. Each of you, in such amazing ways, reminds me why every day I wake with a heart full of gratitude and joy to greet the experiences of the day. You are always with me, and there for me. I could fill an entire book with the many ways you support me! You are journeying with me and knowing you are here with understanding, support, a joke, a challenge, hugs, tears and smiles, adds strength to my purpose. It's easy to show love when I have such beautiful love modeled for me through you. Thank you for you Diana, Cherri, Cheryl, Kathy, Deb, Jeanne, Sue, Arlene, Ginny, Mikki, Dee, Linda, Diane, Carrie Ann, Mavis, Dawn, Rachel, Lora, Klaus, Christel, John, Charles, Bill and Rhonda.

I am gratefully indebted to several people who have been incredibly helpful to me in bringing *Our Journey of Love* to our world. Thank you each so much for the ways you generously taught me what I didn't know, eased my path, created amazing work, and helped this be such an amazing experience that I am now eagerly looking forward to creating my next book.

Mitra Shaffy – Creating the inspired image of the dandelion at seed that began bringing to life the vision of our creation.

Kristin Thompson – I am excited about your continuing to help me bring and share my dreams to our world. Thank you for generously introducing your Tribe to the industry experts you've worked with who also help us bring our dreams to life.

Suzanne Doyle-Ingram – You made the book writing process incredibly straight forward. There was never a moment of overwhelm. You are amazing to work with and I know our journey together has just begun.

Angie Ishak – You are an incredible editor. You helped me make sure my words accurately reflect my intent to help caregivers. You so valuably immersed yourself into the structure, message and impact of my messages.

Heather Mize – You turned my entire book around in the time it would probably have taken me to work on the first page. You are delightful to work with, you asked questions that created a more quality experience for the readers, and your attention to detail is spectacular.

Jim Murphy – We made it! I didn't know how to visually express what was in my heart and you patiently brought me closer and closer. You presented images I didn't know to think of, and you delivered samples almost instantly. I am truly grateful for all you did.

SUSAN J. RYAN

Table of Contents

Foreword

Dear Reader,

I realize this is not a traditional book foreword and yet it is the perfect foreword for this book. The purpose of a book foreword is to introduce you to the book, and to its author.

Cynthia Davis does both so perfectly by capturing the essence of the journey represented by *Our Journey of Love, 5 Steps to Navigate Your Caregiving Journey*. More than this, her inspired letter invites each of us to begin the book as if we are the author of this letter, writing to the person for whom we are providing care. It moves us through our journey from our early stumbles to our place of balance, presence and love.

From Cynthia's foreword, I hope you feel my passion to be your guide, so your journey as a caregiver transitions from perhaps a feeling of overwhelm to being able to, as Cynthia says, "begin each day anew, knowing and trusting that in this precious present moment, YOU ARE ABLE and YOU ARE LOVE."

Susan J. Ryan

"My Dearest Love,

Today I can wake with love in my heart and greet this day with a smile. I know I haven't always been patient, or kind, or very loving or even really present with you, however, now I am learning how! I now have a guide, a roadmap, a mentor and, through her shared experience I am learning to live so far beyond simply coping – I have actually found my joy again!

My joy, our joy, was always there, in my heart. However, all too often I was overtaken by the daunting responsibilities that, like wave after wave, just kept coming at me and I had no idea how to manage it all. My feelings of overwhelm and fear of doing it all wrong consumed me and I lost sight of me – and, more importantly, I lost sight of You. I lost sight of how to love in a situation so far beyond my understanding.

Our friends became distant and it started to feel like our whole world was closing in on us. Rather than living out our dreams of travel, and family gatherings, and dancing until dawn, our world is one of doctors, clinics, clinicians, tests, and more tests. Everyone means well, but it seems like everyone is going through the motions and we became part of "the system".

With each passing day, I live with the feeling of losing you and yet you are here – still needing me. And, at some level, I sense the real you, Your Presence, is still here. And so, my dear, forgive my lack of understanding and please continue to be a bit patient with me as I now take this journey with you. We are starting anew today, together.

You see, this book found its way to me and as I read it, it was as if she knew me and knew you. My dear, I found hope. I learned how to cope and deal with the swirl of emotions and day to day tasks that would consume me --making me feel angry and fearful, overwhelmed and even mad. I began to see a side of me I hardly recognized, and I didn't know how to deal with it. But it's as if she has my back and, given she has traveled this road, our road, she knows my heart and has touched my heart. I am learning how to take things in stride – separating what is really important from the things that can wait. And, more importantly, I am learning how to express my love for you in a new way – it never left, I simply lost my way.

I am not sure I know why this is our journey, and some things may never be revealed in this lifetime, however, I do know, in stepping on the path of Our Journey of Love, I am not alone. Even in our darkest hour, there is hope and I can begin each day anew, knowing and trusting that in this precious present moment, I AM ABLE and I AM LOVE.

So now, let's sleep, my love, tomorrow is a new day!

Cynthia A. Davis
CEO, Radiant Blue, LLC

Introduction

My journey with providing care support began more than thirty years ago. In my first experiences, I felt like I was on an emotional roller coaster—often blindfolded—and not knowing what to expect next. I didn't know anything. I didn't know where to start, I didn't know what to do next, I didn't even know what I didn't know!

I constantly felt overwhelmed. I felt like I was missing something. I was disappointed in myself because I felt like I should be able to do more for the person receiving the specialized care I was providing. The name I use for this person is "care receiver". I didn't think I was providing the best care for my care receiver, and I also didn't even know what that should look like.

I was exhausted mentally, physically and emotionally. I assumed my exhaustion was just part of being a care giver. I lost who I was in giving care. I was only surviving. I didn't like the disease. I didn't like what it was doing to my care receiver, to me, and to those around us. I felt helpless and I didn't like it, so I began to learn.

I still sometimes feel like I'm just beginning to learn. Now, instead of feeling helpless and overwhelmed, I'm filled with hope and love. I feel balanced. I'm incredibly grateful for the wisdom I've gained these past years and I feel good about the care I provide for my care receiver *and* for myself.

If we could write up a list of experiences we wanted to have in our lives, perhaps few of us would sign up for caregiving as part of our journey. This is true for those who give care to someone who has received a disease diagnosis, experienced a traumatic event or live with a specific condition. It is also true for those of us who have received our own disease diagnosis, experienced a traumatic event ourselves, or live every day with our own specific condition.

My vision with *Our Journey of Love: 5 Steps to Navigate Your Caregiving Journey*, is to help everyone in roles of care support positively navigate their journey, the journey of their care receiver, and the journeys of those who support them. My passion, and my belief are that since giving care is part of the experiences in our journey, we are meant to thrive within them, just like experiences we would have chosen. We are meant to discover how to have the most positive experiences throughout our journeys together.

I'm indebted to everyone who teaches, guides, and supports me on my journey, as well as those who hold me accountable for self-care. I am passionately and gratefully called to use what I've learned to help and guide you on your journey. This book is one way I pay my gratitude forward for those who help me. If even one thing I share improves your journey, or the journey of your care receiver, my journey is worth it.

I'm not a doctor and I don't even hint at offering any medical advice. I'm grateful to the doctors and nurses who continue to help my loved ones, and me, navigate our journeys.

I have written *Our Journey of Love: 5 Steps to Navigate Your Caregiving Journey*, in the first person to clearly reflect sharing my story, not to tell you what you need to do. I'm inviting you to consider what I've learned from my experiences, both what has and what has not worked for me. With each of my experiences, I try what I've previously learned and what others offer based on their experiences. I don't assume everything will work or that if it worked in one situation it will work in all situations.

I share stories and examples from my caregiving experiences. Many of these are from my roles of care support for those with types of dementia. These lessons, tips and tricks have also been shared with care givers who are caring/have cared for those with other conditions; they have found them valuable for their circumstances as well.

Throughout *Our Journey of Love*, I reference my husband, Jack. We met in 2001 and married in 2003. He is the love of my life and the man of my dreams. Jack is one of the smartest people I have ever met. He is kind, has a great sense of humor, and lives his life as a model of honesty and ethical behavior. I am blessed to be in his life and have him in mine, and I cherish each second of our lives together. Jack was diagnosed with a type of Dementia in early 2014. He has received three different diagnoses throughout our journey, something I have learned is not uncommon. In October 2017, I moved him into a memory care facility where he gets the care and support that helps him thrive. He is happy and I am very grateful.

The title of this book, *Our Journey of Love*, comes from how I feel about my journeys in roles of care support. What I have learned over the years, and through my experiences, is that even though a disease or significant event may take away pieces of our lives as we knew them, seeds of potential, lessons for how we can improve, and opportunities to help others are planted. I learn about myself from experiences that challenge me and those that delight me.

The concept for the cover art of *Our Journey of Love*, came from the amazing artist, Mitra Shaffy. Yes, the dandelion seeds that represent our memories are blowing away; they are also taking with them potential, lessons, and opportunities to positively touch other lives.

Through the *massive acceptance* and *radical presence* I've learned along this journey, I embrace each insight with an open mind. One of the lessons I've learned is ensuring that I view each experience I have through my own lens, not someone else's. I've learned that this allows me to remain present and focus on what is before me while equipping both my care receiver and me for our best possible experiences.

I give you guidance about what I've learned in many areas including:

- Identifying caregiving roles with clarity.
- Making it easier to handle frustrations (including friends stepping away).
- Creating more positive experiences for you and your care receiver.
- Reducing stress and eliminating overwhelm.
- Having the hard conversations we would rather not have.

I am a person of deep faith. It is an integral component of my life. I respect that faith is an area some people either choose not to embrace or have stepped away from. In *Our Journey of Love*, I rarely include specific references to my faith and appreciate your patience when I do.

I share even more lessons, tips, tricks, and stories on our website: OurJourneyofLove.net.

Note:
The American Psychiatric Association's (APA) Diagnostic and Statistical Manual of Mental Disorders (DSM), is recognized as the authoritative guide to the diagnosis of mental disorders for

health care professionals around the world. Its fifth revision, known as DSM-5, was published in 2013. In it, they changed classifications of Dementia and Alzheimer's Disease.[1]

> Dementia was replaced in DSM-5 because the term was deemed stigmatizing; the rough translation from the Latin roots is "loss of mind." Acknowledging that old habits die hard, however, DSM-5 also states that use of the term is not precluded "where that term is standard." The old DSM-IV category of delirium, dementia, and amnestic and other cognitive disorders has been replaced in the DSM-5 by the neurocognitive disorders category. Major or mild neurocognitive disorder from Alzheimer's disease is included within this new category.[2]

I did significant research on these changes. I applaud the APA's goal to replace stigmatizing names based on their definitions. I incorporate both names in this book because "neurocognitive disorders" has not become widely recognized yet. The APA states they recognize the name "dementia" is already widely used and their new classifications will most likely be used only by health care professionals and related organizations.

Step 1: Coping Mechanisms for the Emotional Roller Coaster

I'm always doing my very best with where I am at.
I find coping mechanisms to support me staying emotionally balanced on my journey.

My emotional roller coaster ride begins.

It was a beautiful May day in Chicago, IL. Neighbors up and down the street came outside to enjoy the feeling of the warm sun, finally without jackets! We were eager to work outside in our yards once again. I had the best neighbors: Bob and Mary. They had been together nearly sixty years and were as loving with each other as they were in their courting days. On this day, Bob was trying to bring a planter onto their porch that was almost as big as he was! I rushed over to help and together we got the planter outside for spring. When we finished, Bob said, "I'm worried about Mary."

This was completely out of the ordinary for Bob, an engineer who delighted in figuring out and solving the tiniest of details. He went on to explain Mary had gotten up in the middle of the night, thought it was time to start preparing the Thanksgiving meal and turned on the oven to preheat their turkey. Bob explained that he would have chalked it up to a dream except that a few days before, Mary got in the car and started driving to the store for groceries. Mary hadn't driven a car for more than ten years.

Bob and Mary's journey was my first experience with the caregiving emotional roller coaster, its impact on their lives, the lives of their family, and the lives of all of us who love them.

At the time, *we didn't know what we didn't know*. Those of us who surrounded Bob and Mary were continuously frustrated. All of us wanted to help and we didn't know how. There was not as much information available then as there is now. None of us had any experience with friends or loved ones who had been formally diagnosed with dementia, and we didn't know about support communities to reach out to at that time. While we all kept talking together and trying anything we thought might help, our underlying emotions were helplessness, anxiety, confusion and frustration. We beat ourselves up for being unable to do more and found ourselves always dreading what would go wrong next. We didn't have the capacity to look for joy or to look for happiness.

In the early days of Mary's diagnosis, she would sometimes have wonderful days when we thought the diagnosis must have been wrong; we felt she must have had something temporary that seemed like dementia and we felt a sense of hope. Then something scary would happen that, for us, was like the plunge on a roller coaster and it took all of us off-balance. Even on her good days, we were waiting for the "other shoe to drop." We were afraid of what Mary might do next and were concerned for Bob. Our emotions were a disruptive blend of helplessness, love, frustration, hope, fear, uncertainty, concern, anxiety, and yes, anger. Our emotions were complex and confusing.

Why did this have to happen to such wonderful and loving people? Why couldn't we figure out how to make it better? How come nothing we did made a difference? We worried as much about Bob as we did about Mary and we never felt a sense of clarity or calm.

Bob, who had taken care of Mary for so many years, was her knight in shining armor and he was adamant he would care for her through this. He was diligent 24/7. We helped him put up baby gates, so Mary could get up in the night to go to the bathroom but not go to any other room or out of the house. Bob always woke up to make sure Mary was safe and that she went back to sleep. That meant he wasn't getting enough sleep. He took on her care along with her former household chores; he saw it as part of their vows of marriage.

One thing that always brought a smile to Mary's face was hearing the music she loved. Bob and Mary had 78RPM records[3] and Bob would play music by artists like Bing Crosby, Benny Goodman, Perry Como and Glenn Miller. We didn't connect how valuable the music was for her at the time; I'm sure if we'd realized it, music would have been playing all the time.

While their three amazing daughters helped in any way Bob would allow, he was steadfast that it was his responsibility to keep Mary at home and take care of her. His daughters and their families would often feel frustrated because they wanted to do so much more for both Bob and Mary and Bob wouldn't let them. He'd say over and over: "Thank you, I love you, I've got this."

When Mary finally passed away, we all had conflicting emotions, especially sadness combined with relief that she wasn't suffering anymore. We felt grief for Bob and his loss, along with hope he could finally get some rest. We felt concern for Bob because he hadn't been taking care of himself. We felt concern for their daughters who grieved the loss of their mother while trying to figure out how to console their father, and how to come to terms with their deep feelings of inadequacy. Throughout Bob and Mary's journey, their daughters kept believing they could have done more.

Can you relate to any part of this story?

The Emotional Roller Coaster of Caregiving

The first time someone explained the journey of caregiving as an emotional roller coaster, I felt like they had painted the perfect picture of what we were going through. While I've always liked riding roller coasters, I hadn't previously considered what I liked about them, or why, so I made a list. I then made a list of the emotions I've felt as I've traveled through each caregiving role. I found the two experiences have a lot in common!

Roller coasters and caregiving both:

- Take us through a wide range of emotions.
- Are not easy physically, emotionally, or mentally.
- Have lots of disruption along their way.
- Require our presence and focus to make it as easy as possible.
- Confuse our brain's fight-or-flight response.

- Cause us to quickly shift from a removed, impersonal view to wanting knowledge as quickly as possible.
- Result in different experiences when we're watching someone else vs. when we're experiencing one.
- Have common elements and each experience is different.

My story about Bob and Mary is a true one. I changed their names, but not the emotional roller coaster of the situation. We didn't accept the journey. We didn't stay present in the experiences. We didn't focus on what we could learn. We didn't take care of ourselves. We constantly projected the worst even though we didn't even know what the worst looked like! We didn't have hope. We didn't consider that our journey had meaning and purpose.

Riding the Roller Coaster Blindfolded

I've experienced an emotional roller coaster in a number of different care roles. With each event, I would let the disease determine my feelings, thoughts, emotions, and actions. This approach was like riding a roller coaster blindfolded. While I had a basic understanding of the situation, I'd be constantly reacting and usually feeling off-balance. This was my experience with Bob and Mary.

Now, even though each caregiving journey is unique, I'm no longer blindfolded. I'm no longer constantly reacting and off-balance. With the lessons I continue to learn, I'm empowered to stay present in what's happening. As situations present themselves, I cope with each component of my care support for what it is. I honor my emotions for what they teach me about myself, allowing them to guide my steps and strengthen my actions. I choose how I am going to act in each moment. I don't judge or blame the disease. I know where and how to find the support resources and information to help me maintain emotional balance and well-being. I now have purpose behind my knowledge and this calls me to share with you in this book the wisdom I've learned and the person I'm becoming.

The journey is constant. I continue to have powerful and valuable lessons along the way that help me with the emotional roller coaster of caregiving. One of these lessons came from a simple comment, yet it transformed my perspective of the emotional roller coaster. It reminds me to be aware of where I am on the roller coaster and allows me to choose my feelings, thoughts, emotions and actions, with intention, so I am able to stay present and emotionally balanced.

What are Coping Mechanisms?

When my dad's behavior began changing in confusing ways, we all became concerned. We had no idea what was causing it. Our speculations included everything from a lack of water intake to a concussion from slipping on the ice one day. No matter what we tried, his symptoms didn't go away, they continued to increase. Among the signs, my mother-in-love, Donna, explained dad was having difficulty completing sentences, remembering what to do next or what he had already completed. This included common everyday tasks. He had begun forgetting how to do tasks he had done for years—like fixing his breakfast—and had begun closing the blinds early in the afternoon. Because I was living in another state, I didn't see his changes. I did begin to notice them during our daily phone conversations.

Many years of my career as a sales representative had included a significant amount of travel, so I was in the habit of calling my parents every night. They wanted to know what city I was in and my dad wanted to talk with me about my various accounts. During our conversations while I was on the road, he must have taken notes because he would regularly ask me very specific questions! We had incredible conversations over the years as my dad continued to teach and challenge me.

My dad's symptoms during our phone conversations began as fumbling for words here and there, progressed to struggling for complete sentences, and advanced to forgetting entire conversations. It became difficult for my dad to talk on the phone—the phone became confusing for him and he couldn't comprehend that it was my voice coming through. I knew the day was fast approaching when I would no longer have our treasured conversations. I became overwhelmed with grief and sadness.

Sobbing, I called a friend to tell her what was happening. She asked me a question I had never been asked or considered on my own: "How are you coping?" *Coping?* I had no idea what coping was. She told me it was time to begin thinking about what coping mechanisms I could start using because my dad's condition would not improve.

I now use coping mechanisms to help me adjust to stressful situations, so I stay balanced and maintain my emotional well-being. These strategies can be conscious or unconscious[4]. I've learned my coping mechanisms are unique to me. What works for me may not work for anyone else and while I want to learn what coping mechanisms others use, they may not work for me. The most important thing I've learned is to continue actively seeking them out, trying them out to see if they work for me, and using the ones that stick!

Coping mechanisms help me deal with the mental or emotional strain or tension resulting from adverse or very demanding circumstances that can alter my emotional balance[5]; the definition of stress. Throughout *Our Journey of Love: 5 Steps to Navigate Your Caregiving Journey*, I introduce coping mechanisms that work for me, why they help me maintain my emotional balance, and how they support my practice of massive acceptance and staying radically present. These all contribute to both my care receiver and me experiencing the best journey we can.

It's Bigger Than Me

How did I cope with giving up the daily calls with my dad? By breaking it down and making the experience bigger than me. I began by asking myself what I could do to allow an easier time for my dad, Donna, and me. What did I want for each of us? I then broke the experience into smaller and smaller components until I could look at it from a place of objectivity and conscious choice, not through the lens of my emotions. I thought about how discontinuing these calls would help ease my dad's experience. I considered what I could to do to ease the situation for Donna. I thought about what I wanted for my own experience. I thought about how this transition impacted all three of us.

My dad wasn't choosing to quit making the calls; the telephone was becoming frustrating and difficult for him to use. I realized I was giving his mind peace by ending our phone conversations and saw this as a gift of love for him and for Donna. Donna didn't want us to stop talking and knew how much those calls meant to both my dad and me. I also knew it would be difficult for her to tell me to stop the phone conversations, so I showed Donna my love of and support for her by calling her to initiate the end of our calls myself.

When that day came, I was able to handle the loss of our emotional connection that had resulted from our calls. When the calls ended, rather than grieve their loss, I honored their memory daily. When I would think of picking up the phone to call my dad, I would instead think of a memory I could smile about. I would say a prayer for him and a prayer for Donna.

Plus, I could still talk with him in my mind.

When I was growing up, my dad taught me to "talk with him" in my mind. He wanted me to learn how to think through situations as though we were talking together. This way, when he was not able to actually talk with me, we could still "work things out" together. Thankfully, I had many years of those memories stored up so even though we ceased our phone conversations, I still had his counsel.

With these intentional decisions, I was able to make conscious choices about my experience rather than unconsciously allowing emotions to control and disrupt me.

My experience with my dad prepared me for when it came time for my husband, Jack, to move into a memory care facility. As Jack's disease progressed, I knew it would soon be time for him to receive a level of care I was not qualified to provide at home. As I had done with discontinuing phone conversations with my dad, I made this experience with Jack bigger than me. I considered what I wanted for Jack, the care facility support teams, our family, and me. I broke down these areas into smaller and smaller components until I could consider each one objectively.

For Jack, my goal was keeping him safe and happy and I knew:

- I wasn't strong enough to lift him if he fell.
- I wasn't strong enough to stop him if, in a "dementia moment," he became aggressive or wanted to leave.
- I wasn't able to provide him a level of social stimulation that was both vital for him and geared towards what was accessible to him.
- I needed to begin preparing him for the time when he would be living alone and in a different environment.

Regarding the care facilities, I spoke with several I was evaluating, asking them about their guidelines for residents so we could prepare Jack and streamline his transition:

- What kind of personal belongings could residents have in their rooms?
- What couldn't residents have because of location or safety rules?
- What were facility practices for personal hygiene?
- What were the care facility support teams' responsibilities?

The facilities didn't allow any sharp objects in the rooms: push pins for photos, manual razors, nail scissors or clippers. Jack had been using a manual razor. I helped him start using an electric razor, using compassionate truth for a few days about being out of razor blades. He soon forgot about the manual razor.

Care facilities use disposable, absorbent undergarments for residents. I thought it might be overwhelming for Jack to adapt to these on top of adapting to his new home, so, while he was still at home, we talked about using "nighttime" underpants so he wouldn't have to get up in the night. I was surprised by how easy it was for Jack to adapt to this. I had anticipated resistance and received none. By the time he moved into the care facility, even though he didn't actually need them, he was already familiar with the disposable undergarments and there was no adjustment.

Sleeping alone. Jack had grown up in a large family. In college, he lived in a fraternity house, in the military, he lived in a barracks. He married as he left the military. He and his first wife, Sue, raised four sons. He wasn't used to living alone. He had only lived on his own after Sue passed away and before we married. I wanted to "teach" him how to sleep alone.

Jack was already used to going to sleep first and I was always there with him. If he got up in the night, so did I. I was there to guide him to the bathroom, back to bed, and make sure he went back to sleep. I began to "teach" him by leaving the bedroom after he first went to sleep at night. I closed the door and began sleeping on the couch that faced our bedroom. I kept lights on in the bathroom so he could see if he got up, and I left him alone in the room.

This was not an easy adjustment for Jack. Sometimes, he would wake up in the night, use the restroom, and go right back to bed. Other times, he forgot what he was doing. When I came into the room in the morning, clothes would be strewn around, or he would be sleeping in our chair; we persisted. He finally got used to it. By the time he was ready to move into memory care, he had learned to sleep alone.

One of the people with whom I shared this story explained she would never give up one moment with her husband. I absolutely respect this. My decisions are what worked for me because, even though I was sad to stop sharing a bed with my husband, I thought of the experience I wanted him to have in the care facility. I knew that in a time in his life when he needed as few disruptions as possible, being disoriented and newly alone in his room would not be helpful for him. This made it the right choice for me. When he moved into the care facility, I received reports of how easily he adapted in these areas.

The experience I wanted for the care team was to make Jack's adjustment as easy as possible so they could focus on his care. What experience did I want for myself? My goal was keeping Jack safe and happy. My ability to take intentional, forward-thinking steps made the transition as smooth as possible for all of us. I have never regretted my choice.

Resilience as a Coping Mechanism

I frequently attend care giver meetings in our community. As with other types of communities, we learn with and from each other. We lean on one another to support, encourage, share, and hug each other. We are part of a comforting place to just "be."

In one of our meetings, I was sharing a caregiving experience about Jack. I explained how much easier it had been, and how much better I felt about the outcome of this experience than when I first experienced something similar with Mary. When I finished sharing, one of the other care givers turned to me and told me I was incredibly "resilient." While I'd heard the word before, I hadn't considered it as an attribute of my personality. With the combination of my unquenchable curiosity, and commitment never to use labels that I don't wholly comprehend, I came home and began to research the meaning of resilience.

Wow! I was truly surprised by what I learned. I searched a variety of websites for their definitions of resilience and what it means in our lives. I realized that, even without intentionally focusing on it, I have become resilient over the years. I had a series of "ah ha" moments as I recognized the importance of resilience in my life, in my roles of care support, and as a coping mechanism. I now see it as a valuable component of my purpose in giving care with love.

Here are some insights about resilience I learned in my research:

- Resilience is not a trait that people have from birth. Resilience involves our feelings, thoughts, emotions, and actions. These can be learned and developed in anyone[6].
- Resiliency can be learned, acquired, and honed through conscious decisions to observe and practice[7].
- Resilience helps me not only bounce back, it helps me learn from my experiences, adapt, and grow, so I am better prepared to manage my next experience.
- Resilience allows me to access the more constructive aspects of this emotional roller coaster. I am aware of my feelings. Because of this I can process and deal with my feelings without allowing them to control me.

The most valuable lesson I learned is that everyone has the ability to become resilient. For me, I realized that I can also support my care receiver in their resilience.

I looked at a variety of dictionaries for definitions of resilience. Here are a few:

- "[The] ability to recover quickly from difficulties or adjust easily to misfortune or change[8]."
- "An individual's capacity to thrive in the face of significant trauma[9]."
- "The ability to be happy, successful, etc. again after something difficult or bad has happened[10]."

While each one of these definitions is slightly different, they collectively represent resilience as my ability to face challenges, adapt successfully, and thrive in my life. This is a trait I now intentionally embrace to improve.

Andy Stanley[11], is the Founder and Senior Pastor of North Point Ministries Inc., in Alpharetta, GA. In some of his messages, he explains that as a pastor, he frequently hears stories of great hardship. Some of the people sharing their stories are struggling tremendously; some are well-adjusted and thriving in their lives. He discovered the common denominator in each of the well-adjusted individuals is "their experiences remind them, but do not define them." They have learned lessons from their experiences, have grown stronger as a result of them, and use their lessons to help others. This is the essence of resilience.

Resilience and Balance

The more resilient I become, the more present I am with my care receiver and the more emotionally balanced I am in my life. The more balanced I am in my life, the more capacity I have to deal with sudden changes from a place of acceptance and presence. When there is a major change and I go from feeling peaceful in our journey to a sudden kick in the gut, I don't go back to the beginning of the roller coaster ride. I take action and quickly bounce back, even stronger.

Here's an example of how resilience helped me stay emotionally balanced during a caregiving experience. My ability to stay completely present also allowed me to incorporate another one of my coping mechanisms—humor. I make reference in this story to what I call "dementia moments." I define these as times when my care receiver and I are unable to relate rationally and trying to respond logically won't help. Accepting these moments for what they are allows me to stay balanced when they happen.

As my husband, Jack's, Alzheimer's disease progresses, he recalls experiences in his life differently than how they actually occurred and he doesn't remember his normal routines. His nighttime routine is an example. One night, I couldn't get Jack to go to bed. I tried everything I could think of and finally decided to see if me going to bed first would help. I felt safe trying this because I'd gotten a double key deadbolt on our front door, which meant there was no way he could accidentally leave the house. I got myself ready and went to bed (constantly looking at the door and listening for any sounds). About twenty minutes later, Jack walked into our room and stood at the foot of our bed. I asked him if he was ready to come to bed, and he asked, "Who are you?" I realized he was in a "dementia moment" and had no idea who I was. I told him I was his wife, Sue. He replied, "No, you're not. And I'm not sleeping with anyone who isn't my wife."

I wisely got out of bed, calmly apologized to him for the inconvenience, peacefully walked out of the room, quietly closed the door and lay down on the couch facing our bedroom. I was also jumping for joy inside because, even in the middle of a "dementia moment," my precious husband was still moral and ethical! Early in my caregiving journey, I would have had a completely different emotional experience.

Previously, I would have been sad that my husband didn't recognize me. I would have felt confused and helpless, with no ideas about what to do or who to ask for help. I would have been resentful—why did this have to happen? I would have been frustrated and overwhelmed, thinking, *"I'm exhausted, I still have lots to do and I was planning on getting things done when he went to bed. Now I'll have to stay up much later."*

How did this situation end? About fifteen minutes later, our bedroom door opened, and my husband walked over to where I was laying down. His "dementia moment" had passed. He asked me what I was doing there and when I was coming to bed. By staying completely present and emotionally balanced, he stayed calm, too. In Steps 3 and 5, I'll share how I use experiences like this one to continue to prepare me for what's next.

My caregiving journeys *are* emotional roller coasters. I'm already on the roller coaster and it's not going back even if I want it to, so I'm going to do everything I can to make the best of our experiences and help my care receivers have their best experience as well. I can learn to take the ride instead of it taking me. The more I learn, the sooner my blindfold is removed and the smoother my ride becomes. The resilience I develop on our journey helps me improve my experience and that of my care receivers.

Roller Coaster Stages, Resilience, and Rubber Bands

While reading the definition of resilience below, I visualized a rubber band as a metaphor for resilience:

> "The ability of a substance or object to spring back into shape; elasticity[12]."

Rubber bands are elastic, meaning they are designed to stretch and then spring back into shape. This is incredibly valuable for me because when I'm in a caregiving experience, I think of a rubber band and ask myself what state it's in, from its original, relaxed shape to being twisted and stretched so far it's ready to break. This visual gives me clarity about which stage of the caregiving emotional roller coaster I'm experiencing.

From the beginning of my care support journey, I've felt a range of emotions. On reflection, I realize my emotions fall into four stages. The transition from one stage to the next is based on how well I'm able to practice acceptance and be fully present in my journey.

My four stages and corresponding rubber band analogies:

Awakening:
My awakening is quite emotionally charged. I am unbalanced in my experiences and not supported with positive emotions. In this stage, the rubber band is tightly twisted and stretched so far it is about to break.

Awareness:
As I continue my journey, I begin discovering resources and learning lessons. I become aware of hope, become more accepting, begin to adapt to my journey, and have access to positive emotions. In this stage, the rubber band is not as tight and not as twisted.

Conscious Choice:
When I gain clarity, chose my perspective, and engage with communities of people who lean in with understanding and support, I begin making conscious choices. In this stage, the rubber band is still stretched somewhat and it is no longer twisted.

Resilience:
Connecting with my purpose and meaning and practicing massive acceptance and radical presence strengthens my

resilience. In this stage, the rubber band has returned to its original state.

Stages of the Caregiving Emotional Roller Coaster

Awakening

Angry
Confused
Disrupted
Frustrated
Helpless
Overwhelmed
Resentful
Uncertain
Sad
Self-doubt
Self-pity
Selfish Stuck

Rubber band: tightly twisted and
stretched so far it is about to break

Awareness

Accepting
Adapting
Coping
Curious
Guilty
Hope
Kind-hearted
Lost
Relief
Sometimes Okay
Sometimes Sad
Uncertain
Uneasy

Rubber band: not as tightly
twisted or as stretched

Conscious Choice

Compassionate
Connected
Creative
Emotional balance
Empathetic
Grateful to others
Permitted to be happy
Perspective
Positive
Present
Sometimes Sad

Rubber band: still slightly stretched
and it is no longer twisted

Resilience

Calm
Empowered
Engaged
Giving back
Inspired
Peaceful
Purpose
Self-love
Sometimes Sad
Thriving
Well-being
Wise

Rubber band: has returned to its
original relaxed state

My experiences with Bob and Mary would definitely be the first stage, visually represented with a rubber band stretched and tightly twisted until it was about to break! My experience with Jack not remembering who I was in the moment would be in stage three, visually represented by a rubber band still stretched and no longer twisted.

Step 2: I Don't Know What I Don't Know

This is my journey. Beliefs are my compass.
Intention is my guide.
Self-care is my fuel.
I only get lost if I travel someone else's journey.

My first question after Jack and I received the news of his diagnosis: "Where do I begin?"

What I wish the first response would have been: "Breathe! You're not alone. Yes, there is a lot to do and a lot to learn. We're here to help you. Let's not try to think of everything, let's just start with one thing and go from there."

Have you ever seen—or been part of—""blowing machine" contests? You stand in a clear enclosure and pieces of paper start blowing around wildly. They can be money, gift certificates, vouchers. The goal is to grab as many as you can and you get to keep whatever you catch. The pieces are blowing around wildly, bouncing off you and the edges of the machine. There's no order, it's very hard to grab any of the pieces and just when you think you've got one, it goes a different direction. The experience is exhausting and definitely not calm or organized. Think of the pieces in the machine as all the things you need to know and do in your caregiving role.

Why do people go into these machines? Because no matter what they grab onto, they are better off than before they started. After my first caregiving role with Bob and Mary, I knew that even though there was so much I didn't know, I was at least starting somewhere. I would be better off than if I just let everything blow around wildly.

I believed there would come a day when I could slow down the "blowing machine" so I could grab onto more pieces. I focused on realizing the day when I could unplug the "blowing machine" and, even if I didn't understand all the pieces, I could look at them and make conscious choices about what to do with each one.

I chose to start by defining my role in each care support experience.

Who I Am

Caregiver vs. Care giver

When I first began giving care support to someone, I knew I wasn't a "Caregiver." This was a professional title for those who have been formally trained and are paid for their services. They were trained to give specialized care, and they wore uniforms that represented their role as a professional.

I am incredibly grateful for those of you who are professional caregivers. I am in awe of you, humbled by you, and have boundless respect for you. Thank you.

It wasn't until someone told me I was a caregiver that I even considered the term in the context of what I was doing. While I'm not formally trained, I absolutely do want to do everything I can to positively help those for whom I care. I study continuously to improve my knowledge.

In whatever I was learning, and in all support discussions, everything was combined under the title "caregiver." Over the years I have provided multiple types of care for individuals who are no longer able to perform the critical tasks of personal or household care necessary for everyday survival. This is the formal definition of the role of a caregiver[13]. If anyone asked, it would have been easy for me to call myself a caregiver. The challenge I had with this is it *did* put everything I was doing under the umbrella of one word: caregiver.

There is so much to do as a caregiver. I realized I wasn't thinking about each of the caregiving responsibilities I had accepted individually. When I thought about caregiving, I was thinking of all my responsibilities collectively, everything that needed to be done. I was both doing it all and feeling like I *should* be doing it all. This was part of what was causing me to feel overwhelmed.

I began to look at how I could break down my caregiving responsibilities into more manageable tasks so I could feel less overwhelmed and make wise decisions. Now, in each care experience, I separate areas where I provide or receive support, define what kind of support it is, and who is best qualified to provide the support.

While I may be providing care in multiple roles at the same time, I'm not overwhelmed looking at the entirety of care support. I compartmentalize each area of care, so I am able to focus specifically on each need individually. This way, I am able to clearly:

- Observe my care receiver.
- Make wise choices.
- Communicate with others.
- Identify what type of information I need.
- Prioritize how I invest my time.
- Identify, or get help identifying, who is best qualified to provide the care.

I have created my own definitions for the different roles of care I provide. Some of my reasons for this are:

- I'm able to make it very clear that I am not a professional. I do not set that level of expectation with myself and I don't imply it to anyone else.
- There is more than one valuable way care is provided and it doesn't all have to come from me.
- I know my abilities, capabilities, strengths and weaknesses. I give myself permission to be the best me I can be. I don't try to handle care in areas I'm not qualified, and I don't apologize for not doing everything.
- I'm very clear about the type of care I am and am not providing.
- I know the parameters of my responsibilities, and the responsibilities of others involved in the care experience.
- I know what kinds of expertise I need to find for the areas I'm less qualified.

My professional career was in a different field. When looking at career choices, roles in the field of health care and caregiving were not among the options I considered. In order for me to make the clear distinction between what I do and what others do, whether or not they are professionals, I separate the words of each role. For example, I am a "care giver" not a "caregiver." I combine this with the specific definition of each of the roles I am serving. This way, everyone who is participating in roles of support for my care receiver clearly knows the boundaries and responsibilities of our roles. This simplifies communications, reduces overwhelm, and ultimately helps our care receiver, and us, have our best experiences.

I've shared my distinctions with many people over the years who are professional Caregivers, and others who, like me, began providing care for someone without it being our previous consideration or choice of profession. Each individual has understood, and most have agreed with, my distinctions. I'm sharing them here for your consideration.

I used dictionaries as the foundation for my definitions below. I begin by defining each word in the types of care support and then define each role.

Definitions for Types of Care Support

Care: I care about you. I watch you with serious attention and consideration to make sure I do what is right and good for you to be safe. In everything I do, my intention is to focus on what is in your best interest. I maintain objectivity so I make wise choices. I can't control your happiness. I do everything I can to create the environment for you that supports your happiness[14].

Buddy/Community: Someone, or a group, with whom I can be transparent and vulnerable. A person or group I reach out to for support when I find myself out of balance.

Giver: I give care to you with the pure intention of my very best for you[15].

Guide: I share what I have learned and continue to learn, with the intent of giving you, someone else in a role of giving care, the opportunity to consider any of it for your journey. I don't tell you what to do. I strive to be a model of my beliefs. My intent as your guide is to help your experiences become the best journey for you, your care receiver, and those around you[16].

Partners: We are two or more people who have a special relationship working together to provide the best experiences for our care receiver. We're in this together. I respect you. I place the result of our partnership, our care receiver's best care, as the highest priority of our relationship. I am open-minded about what we agree to work on together and how we agree to have care provided for our care receiver. I consider everything you want to do, even if I don't agree with it. I am honest with myself and with you. If I have any issues, I address them with you directly and without judgement[17].

Primary: I accept responsibility, and I am the first point of contact for specific areas of my care receiver's medical, legal, and lifestyle decisions. I may be an individual, several individuals, members of a family, or a legal team. I accept primary responsibility for all areas of care it has been agreed I am most qualified, and I have the capacity to provide. My goal is always to ensure the best care is being provided for my care receiver for their safety, and for them to be in an environment that supports their happiness. I am honest with myself. If I am unsure, I seek guidance to determine if I am the most qualified person to have primary responsibility for a specific care area. I make wise choices.

Receiver: The person who is receiving specialized care. Sometimes it's the person who has received a disease diagnosis, experienced a traumatic event, or lives with a specific condition. Sometimes it's the person in other roles of care. Sometimes it's a friend or loved one who wants to know how they can help. Sometimes it's me. The reason I don't use the description loved one, even for my husband, is it is important for me to maintain objectivity when making the decisions that are in my care receiver's best interest.

Supporter: I encourage you in your role of care. I'm here when you want someone to talk with, cry with, or celebrate with. I perhaps give you peace of mind through making sure you know you are never alone, 24/7. I don't proactively guide you[18].

Self: Me. I keep sight of who I am, how I feel, what's important to me, what I need, and how I care for myself. I remember caring for myself is my greatest form of love. This is not being selfish, it's being purposeful. I remember my care receiver doesn't want me to lose myself. When I'm my best me, I am my best for others[19].

Definitions of Roles of Care Support

Here is where I bring together the components of the roles of care support I identified above. These clarify how and why I use the two words for the definitions of the roles.

Care Buddy/Community: I am an individual, or a group, who you, someone who provides care, can be transparent and vulnerable with. You reach out to me for support and guidance when you find yourself out of balance. I care about you. I watch you with serious attention and consideration to make sure I do what is right and good for you to be safe. In everything I do, my intention is to focus on what is in your best interest. I can't control your happiness. I do everything I can to create the environment for you that supports your happiness.

Care Giver: I care about you. I provide your care in the areas where I, and the primary care giver or care partners, have agreed I am most qualified. I watch you with serious attention and consideration to make sure I do what is right and good for you. I maintain objectivity so I am able to make wise choices. I can't control your happiness. I do everything I can to create the environment for you that supports your safety and happiness. I get help from qualified professionals when I'm not the best resource.

Care Guide: This book is an example of my being a care guide. I care about you. I am focusing with serious attention and consideration on what I am sharing to make sure I do what is right and good for you. I maintain objectivity so I am able to make wise choices. In everything I do, my intention is to focus on what is in your best interest. I can't control your happiness. I do everything I can to create the environment for you that supports your happiness. I'm sharing what I have learned, and will continue to share lessons I learn, with the intent of giving you, someone else in a role of giving care, the opportunity to consider using any of it in your journey. I don't tell you what to do. I model my beliefs. My intent as a guide is to help your journey be the best experience for you, your care receiver, and those around you.

Care Partners: We care about each member of our team. We work together and share responsibility for the person we are partners in care with, so they are safe and in the environment that supports their happiness. Our intent with our relationship is to help our journey be the best experience for our care receiver, and for each of us. We maintain objectivity so we are able to make wise choices. As a team, we determine, and agree on, which areas each of us accepts responsibility for. We discuss major decisions before making them and we communicate frequently. We respect each other; each of us places the result of our partnership - our care receiver's best care - as the highest priority of our relationship. We are open-minded to what we work on together and how we work. We consider everything our team members want, even if we don't agree. We can't control each other's happiness. We are honest with ourselves. If we have any issues, we address them together directly and without judgement.

Care Receiver: I care about you. I watch you with serious attention and consideration to make sure I do what is right and good for you to be safe. In everything I do, my intention is to focus on what is in your best interest. I maintain objectivity so I am able to make wise choices. I can't control your happiness. I do everything I can to create the environment for you that supports your happiness, the person who is receiving the care I'm offering in the moment. You may have a disease diagnosis, have experienced a traumatic event, or live with a specific condition in your life. Sometimes you are the person in roles of caring. Sometimes you're a friend or loved one who wants to know how they can help. Sometimes it's me.

Care Supporter: I care about you in your role of care. I'm here when you want someone to talk with, cry with, celebrate with. I perhaps give you peace of mind through making sure you know you are never alone - 24 x 7. I don't proactively guide you. I can't control your happiness. When you ask for my support, I do everything I can to create the environment for you that supports your happiness. I encourage you in your role of care. In everything I do, my intention is to focus on what is in your best interest.

Primary Care Giver: I care about you, my care receiver. My goal is always to ensure you are being provided the best care for your safety. I watch you with serious attention and consideration to make sure I do what is right and good for you to be safe. In everything I do, my intention is to focus on what is in your best interest. I maintain objectivity so I am able to make wise choices. I can't control your happiness. I do everything I can to create the environment for you that supports your happiness. I give to you with the pure intention of my very best for you. I accept responsibility, and I am the primary point of contact for, specific areas of your medical, legal, and lifestyle decisions it has been agreed I am most qualified, and I have the capacity to provide. I may be an individual, several individuals, members of a family, or a legal team. I am honest with myself. If I am unsure, I seek guidance to determine if I am the most qualified person to have primary responsibility for a specific care area. I make wise choices.

Self-Care: I care about me. I provide my primary care in the areas where I'm qualified. I watch myself with serious attention and consideration to make sure I do what is right and good for me. I accept responsibility for medical and legal decisions. I do everything I can to create the environment for me that supports my safety and happiness. I get help from qualified professionals when I'm not the best resource. I keep sight of who I am, what's important to me, how I feel, what makes me unique, what I need, how I care for myself. I remember caring for myself is my greatest form of love, it's not selfish. I remember my care receiver doesn't want me to lose myself. When I'm my best me, I am my best for others.

Throughout my caregiving journey, I've learned I'm usually in multiple roles in the same journey. For example, with my Dad, I was a care partner and a care supporter. His wife Donna was his primary care giver. I supported Donna in her journey. I didn't offer her advice proactively; if she reached out, I was always there and did everything I could to encourage her. In my journey with my husband Jack, Donna is now one of my care supporters; she's always there for me.

I am Jack's primary care giver. Now that he is living in a memory care facility, I am also his care partner for the team who now manage his daily care. I am the care supporter for those who love and want to share time with him. I practice self-care so I am my best version of myself in all my other roles.

Who I'm Not

When I became a care giver, I thought I would immediately become an expert. Wrong! In my early experiences, I didn't have an abundance of resources readily available so I "assumed" I should be able to figure it out. I also didn't have someone else who looked at me and asked, "What are you thinking?!"

My proverbial "whack upside the head" came one day when I was updating my professional résumé, something my dad taught me to do every couple of years. I did this so I stayed current with what I had accomplished and could more easily look at where I wanted to be. I realized if I had applied for a position as a professional caregiver, my application would not have been considered. I had no formal training or background and very little experience. Why would I think I should be either qualified, or almost instantly expert, in any role of giving care?

I made a list of several items for consideration to identify how naturally qualified I am for the role(s) I accept and how committed I am in becoming an expert. Every job interview in which I've participated includes questions about my limitations or areas of improvement. I included these, too!

- From my personal background, what qualifies me as an expert care giver?
- From my professional background, what qualifies me as an expert care giver?
- What past caregiving experiences qualify me as an expert care giver?
- How do my emotions qualify me as an expert care giver?
- How do my emotions disqualify me as an expert care giver?
- Which of my hobbies/interests qualify me as an expert care giver?
- How do my personality, skills and abilities qualify me as an expert care giver?
- How do my personality, skills and abilities disqualify me as an expert care giver?

I know many people who began their caregiving roles early in life, usually with family members. They worked specifically and directly in roles of support. To all of you, thank you for your care. You bring many lessons, tips and tricks that you've learned to your current experiences. However, this wasn't the experience of my own childhood. I didn't have any personal experience with roles of giving care. When I heard stories of families who cared for their loved ones, I remember feeling proud of them and not especially curious about, or interested in, their journey.

As I mentioned previously, my early career choice was not in health care service. I studied hard in school about a variety of subjects, none of which included roles of care support. My hobbies and interests don't include contributing in roles of care support. At the same time, I am naturally empathetic, other-directed and compassionate, so the roles of care support are emotionally comfortable for me. A quote from the Dalai Lama is a great daily affirmation I use.

If you want others to be happy, practice compassion. If you want to be happy, practice compassion[20].

In my roles of care support, I frequently felt that I was a failure, especially when I couldn't figure out what to do for my care receiver. I was very hard on myself! It didn't occur to me to consider that it took me years to become an expert in both my hobby and my profession. I was unfair to myself expecting I'd be an expert in care support in a very short period of time.

The moral of my story is: Please be very kind to yourself when you take on one or more roles of care support. Take a look at the list above and consider asking yourself:

1. How naturally qualified am I for the role(s) I am accepting?
2. How committed am I to becoming an expert in my role(s)?

Accepting the role(s) doesn't translate into instant qualification, passion for the role, and/or expertise in the role. For me, doing this exercise gives me permission to accept myself for who I am rather than who I think I "should" be.

Please don't "should" on yourself. Don't think you "should" be able to handle everything just because _____. (Fill in the blank with whatever is your "just because.") For example, just because "you're successful in your work," just because "your care receiver is your spouse," or just because "you have time." Please figure out the care support areas for which you are best suited and the areas where it's in everyone's best interest to get support from a different resource.

One of the greatest things about having an abundance of support resources available is that when we need help, it's easier to find it. We can then learn more quickly and get helpful ideas when we're stuck.

Who else am I not? I'm not someone who came into this world with an instruction manual for every possible experience I might encounter. Even with all the resources available, sometimes what I try isn't going to work, and sometimes I'm still not the best person to provide all the care.

I have incredible respect for everyone who cares for someone else in any and all capacities. I quite frequently hear that the spouse, children, siblings, and/or other family members are handling all the care because that person is their loved one, and they should be able to handle it because they are family.

If that's the right and best choice, good for you; I support you. I ask you to please intentionally evaluate what areas of care you're best able to provide and work together to figure out which areas need additional help and support resources. Handling it all when it's not the best thing to do can cause sickness and feeling overwhelmed and lead to compassion fatigue, something I address in Step 5. It can diminish the quality of your care receiver's experience. Even though it's done from a place of love, that doesn't automatically make it the best option.

All in the Family

My grandmother was a very strong woman. She owned a business when few women did. She was the president of the state association for her industry when there were almost no women in the industry itself. She absolutely told it like it was; we never wondered what she thought or how she felt about something!

When she was diagnosed with Alzheimer's, she wanted to maintain the normalcy of her life as much as she could. She wanted to stay in her home and she wanted to maintain her routine. My aunt, uncle, and nephew lived nearby and agreed to honor her wishes. They continued to modify their schedules to provide the level of care my grandmother wanted and/or needed. My uncle noticed he periodically felt depressed but didn't think much about it. He didn't relate it to the experience of caring for his mother, something he was glad to do.

As my grandmother's abilities with her daily chores diminished, my uncle stepped up his level of care. My grandmother was petite. My uncle is larger and very strong. Because he was strong, he began lifting her, moving her, bending to get her. He noticed he began having aches and pains, the depression was stronger, and he was exhausted.

My aunt and uncle brought in a home health care nurse to give them guidance about what they should do. She was very helpful and firm. She explained that being strong enough doesn't mean you know what you're doing. She was professionally trained to know how to bend, lift, and carry people. She was also able to clearly explain to him about the other changes he was experiencing.

While their hearts were in the right place, they weren't the best qualified resources to provide all the care my grandmother needed. With the support of a professional, they were able to honor my grandmother's wishes and she was able to stay home until her death.

Who I Can Be

I Don't Have to Walk a Mile to Walk a Mile in Their Shoes

One of the most powerful and most transformative experiences I've had in all my years of giving care was when I experienced an Alzheimer's simulation room. I had no preparation; I had no idea what to expect. Thick gloves were put on my hands, simulating my loss of dexterity. I stepped into slippers that simulated the nerve agitation that commonly occurs in the feet. I don't want you to experience it through my explanation, so I'm not going to share any more of the details.

My respect for anyone struggling with challenges of any kind skyrocketed. Both my empathy and compassion grew stronger. For the first time, the disease wasn't someone else's, it was mine. We were on the same journey together.

Several years before this experience, I had participated in a fundraising walk for a blindness and vision loss non-profit with a group of friends. Each of us wore a pair of glasses that simulated a different type of vision impairment. It was a powerful and transformative experience. Each of us had different simulation glasses and as we walked together, we exchanged glasses so we could experience the different challenges people with these impairments lived with every day. We literally "walked a mile in their shoes."

Whatever type of challenge the person you are caring for is facing, I encourage you to "walk a mile in their shoes," whether through simulators or other methods. On page 169, I've included links to several of the many types of simulation exercises available.

Who I Won't Be

I won't be Living Someone Else's Journey

During my career in sales, I've learned how vitally important it is for me to clearly understand what someone else means when they use labels, their definitions of the words they are using. These labels describe issues and things. My assumption that someone else's definition is the same as mine can result in the loss of relationships and opportunities. Gaining clarity is a sign of respect; When I clearly understand someone else, I am able to serve them in the best possible way. It's an important reason to for me to stay radically present. When I listen carefully, I make sure I understand what someone else means. It's equally important for me to clarify my own definition and understanding of words I use. This way, I am able to clarify my understanding with them to make sure we're in agreement. I'm able to have authentic feelings, thoughts, emotions, and actions. We're both able to have our most positive outcomes.

Definitions Clarify, Labels Mislead

If I don't gain clarity on the words both others and I are using, and I'm using a label for something I don't clearly understand, it stops me from action or may cause me to take the wrong action. It's especially important for me to make sure my care receiver and I are using the same definitions. One example of this in my role of care support was when my care receiver said he wanted to go home. The first time I was told this, we were sitting in our family room, in our home. In my rational mind, we were home so I naively said, "We *are* home." After several failed attempts on my part and a very agitated experience for my care receiver, we survived—poorly—through this experience. The next day, I shared my experience with our support group. There, I was taught one of those lessons that would never have occurred to me on my own!

I was told the story of a care giver whose loved one, their care receiver, had begun saying they wanted to "go home." Just as I had no idea in the beginning, the care giver didn't either. The couple had another home up north, where they had lived for many years. Thinking this was the "home" to which their loved one wanted to go, the care giver packed them up and drove there. When they got to their northern home, their loved one again said they wanted to "go home."

The lesson I learned here is that for our care receivers, "home" is not always our physical home that has an address. "Home" is where they feel safe. I was taught the best way to understand what "home" means is to ask my care receiver to describe it. Agree with them when they describe it. Continue asking questions to learn what "home" means to them in that moment. Once I learned what words represented my care receiver's description of home, I used them to describe the physical place we were, or where we were headed. I now proactively ask my care receiver to describe "home" for me so I make sure the words I use still mean "home" for him. I also practice this regularly for the requests of my care receiver in all areas. In Step 3, I describe a redirection tactic to help care receivers reset their definition of "home" as a physical location.

There is another component of labels I've found equally as important. This is labels I can give or embrace about people, conditions or diseases. These labels prevent me from my best relationship and the negative impact of these can be serious and long-lasting.

A Can Unlabeled

When I was in grade school, my mom would greet me when I got home from school. She would fix me a snack, and we would talk about my day at school. These were great times where she would ask me questions that, while I didn't realize it at the time, were asked to help me process my experiences so I could learn from them.

While I don't remember what the exact reference was, I clearly remember one day when I told my mom about someone my girlfriend had pointed out at school. I used the label for this girl that my friend had used when describing her, even though I hadn't met her. I remember my mom asking me why I thought that described her, and I told her it was because that's what my friend said.

My mom got up from where we were sitting at the kitchen table, went to the cabinet where we stored our canned goods, took out two cans, and brought them back to the table. One of the labels had been removed. My mom asked me to read everything on the label of the can that still had its label. Once I did, she asked me what I thought was in the can and why. She then asked me how I would know if the label was correct. I said we'd have to open the can to make sure.

Mom then handed me the can without the label. She asked me to tell her what was in the can. I said I had no idea because there wasn't a label. She asked me how I would know what was in the can. I said we'd have to open the can to make sure.

The takeaway I learned from that object lesson was simple to me as a child. It has continued to become richer and more valuable to me as an adult. Whether or not someone uses a label (for themselves or for others), it's up to me to discover for myself and create my own understanding and my own definition.

It is easy for me to accept the labels others assign to a disease, its progression and the people with the diagnoses. I don't want to miss opportunities to maximize our experiences because I am looking at them through the lens of someone else's labels.

Even with this, I learned a valuable lesson I will not repeat If I can help it.

I didn't realize I had put experts on a different level. I accepted what they said when they talked about our diagnoses. I learned not to assume the person using the label, even when they are someone regarded as an expert, has the same label definition as me. While I may not like every experience of my journey, it's going to be authentically mine. I give a very clear example of this in Step 3.

It's important for my care receiver and me to talk together about definitions until we both understand each other clearly. It's then easier for both of us to navigate the experiences of our journey together. Practicing massive acceptance of our journey and practicing radical presence in it, with mutual understanding, supports both of us having our best experiences.

Clarity Creates Authenticity

When I hear a word that's important and I don't have a clear definition based on its context, I first ask the person who used it for their definition. Sometimes that's all it takes. If their definition doesn't make sense to me, even if they are an expert, I now look up definitions of the word, and get clarity about that definition.

Worry, Guilt, and Sorry

In my roles of care support, three frequently used words really epitomize why it's so important for me to have understanding and clarity of a definition. These words are *worry*, *guilt*, and *sorry.*

Whenever I'm speaking with a group of people and bring up the words *guilt* and *guilty*, I ask them to share their definition with me. This, by the way, is a great way for you to test yourself on words you use so you make sure you are clear about whether you are using a label someone else defined or you have your own definition. If you're very clear and comfortable with your definition, great. If not, consider researching and coming up with the definition that is clear to you and represents what you want to express.

So far, no one I've asked has had the correct definition of guilt.

Before you read their definitions below, consider first writing down how you define these three words for yourself:

Worry:

_____

Guilt:

_____

Sorry:

_____

Worry:
When I research words, I use several different dictionaries and a thesaurus. Here's an example of one set of definitions for the word worry[21]:

- A state of anxiety and uncertainty over actual or potential problems.
- (To) give way to anxiety or unease; allow one's mind to dwell on difficulty or troubles.

Worry stops my action. When I'm in a "state of anxiety and uncertainty" I'm not focusing on figuring out what I can be doing. Worry doesn't encourage me to take action. When I worry about what I have no control over, I project what might be in the future. I keep coming up with scenario after scenario in my imagination and my level of worry increases. This prevents me from being present to decide on a wise course and take action.

Worry is a wasted emotion that sucks energy from the universe and adds no value.

There is a quote by famed author, humorist, entrepreneur, publisher and lecturer, Mark Twain, I've found very true for me in my life that helps me now search for the emotion that best serves what is going on so I can take productive action.

I've had a lot of worries in my life, most of which never

happened[22].

If I catch myself worrying, I:

- Become aware that I *am* worrying. I worried many years without considering a different solution, so it's still a natural emotion for me to feel at first.
- Ask myself if worry is the emotion that best serves what is going on and, if not, ask myself what emotion serves me in this situation.
- Make sure what I'm worrying about is really the issue or if there is something else going on that shows up as worry in this situation.
- Stay present to exactly what is going on and not project onto the situation. I learned that when I'm anxious about something it's because I'm trying to make a past experience become what's happening rather than staying present and experiencing what actually is happening right now. My anxiousness is my mind's way of telling me it's not right to project what happened in the past onto what's happening now. This prevents me from maximizing the potential of the experience – whether it's positive or challenging.
- Separate my emotions from what's causing my concern so I can think rationally and choose the appropriate emotion.
- Break down my concern into smaller and smaller pieces until I can identify what I actually have any control over. This event begins and ends with me.
- Evaluate what I know I can do and where I need support.
- Get it out in the open and engage with others who can help.
- Take positive action with what I can control.
- Identify how I will know when the situation is resolved.

This insightful quote about worry by author, professor, and motivational speaker, Leo Buscaglia, helps me put the emotion of worry in perspective,

Worry never robs tomorrow of its sorrow, it only robs today of its joy[23].

Guilt:
The definition of guilt is: The fact of having committed a specified or implied offense or crime[24].

Synonyms for the word guilt include:

Culpable, remorse, fault, failing, wrong, wickedness, shame, regret, liability, responsibility, dishonor.

Here are a few of the common ways I hear people talk about guilt in their roles of care support. Does "guilty" seem to you like the best word to use?

I feel guilty going to have lunch with my friends when _____ has to stay home.

I feel guilty having fun when _____ is going through this.

I feel guilty getting my nails done; I should be taking care of _____.

If I'm not using a definition that serves me, how can I have an authentic experience? I ask myself if a word accurately describes what I'm feeling and, if so, why is it the right word? If it's not, I ask myself what I want to feel. *What word/phrase aligns with that feeling? What action(s) can I take so I have the best opportunity of success for my experience?*

For example, instead of "guilty," perhaps it feels "awkward" going to lunch with my friends when _____ has to stay home. I can do something about feeling awkward. I can tell my friends I'm feeling awkward about being away from _____ while we're together, that I've felt like I shouldn't go out and enjoy time with friends when _____ can't do the same thing. I've found that friends understand, lean in to support me, and will help me enjoy our lunch.

What experience do I want? I want to feel good about going to lunch with my friends. I want to be able to stay present with them and focus on our time together. With this clarity, I know what I need to do so _____ is going to be okay while I'm at lunch, and I take specific actions to prepare for this outcome.

Sorry:
When I was a child, if I hit my brother, provoked or not, my parents told me to apologize for doing wrong. I was told to say "I'm sorry" to him and I was almost always punished for doing something I shouldn't have. One time, I was playing dodge ball at school and accidentally hit someone square in the face; I felt awful. I told her I was sorry and asked what I could do to help her. I hadn't meant to hurt her and I took ownership of my responsibility for injuring her.

According to its dictionary definition, when I am sorry[25] about something, I am acknowledging and taking ownership of doing something wrong. The definition of sorry includes feeling regret, remorse, shame, scorn, ridicule, an unpleasant state, and feeling bad because I have caused trouble, suffering or difficulty for someone.

Once I recognized this, I began asking myself if sorry is the word that best represents how I feel every time I use it, especially when I hear someone has received a disease diagnosis, experienced a traumatic event, or lives with a specific condition. Am I responsible in any way? What more accurately represents how I feel?

I've learned that about 95% of my cognitive activity (decisions, actions, emotions, behaviors) happens outside my conscious awareness[26]. I became so used to saying I was sorry about something negative that happened to others, that it became my automatic response. I didn't stop to think about what I truly felt and what I really wanted to say. As my automatic response, I wasn't really focusing on how I wanted to act, feel, think and behave. I wasn't being intentional about my engagement and I underserved the potential of the experience for everyone involved.

I have a dear friend who was recently diagnosed with cancer. I caught myself before saying "I'm sorry." I'm not responsible for causing his disease and I don't owe him an apology. However, I *do* want to help! The most important thing I can do is be conscious of what I'm feeling and what I have capacity to do to provide help. I didn't tell him I was sorry, I told him I'd be there for him and talked with him about areas where he can use help.

Evaluating the words I'm using to make sure they accurately reflect what I mean, and being intentional about my engagement with others, enables me to authentically maximize the potential of my support for them. It also holds me accountable for making sure I'm both taking action and taking the appropriate action.

Sometimes it's not clear how I can help, so I send notes, cards, an emoji, something that authentically represents that I am thinking of them and supporting them. Sometimes I know something specific I can do to help and I ask if I can. We had a friend whose husband had a stroke and their children were flying in. Several of us took turns going to the airport to pick them up and stock up the groceries in their apartment. We were able to focus on a positive contribution.

I've experienced people's discomfort many times over the years when they don't know what to say or do. They almost always, as did I, start with, "I'm sorry." I've learned that by consciously considering how I feel about something, I express how I truly feel. I've also learned to help others who don't know what to say in order to ease their discomfort.

I don't use anyone else's labels if they don't fit. I'm intentional about what I say, how I feel, and how I act. I'm authentically living my journey!

Friendships: Learning About Ourselves and Others

Just like most of us are not professional Caregivers and may not have clarity on how we will think, act, and feel during times of heightened and potentially unfamiliar emotions, our friends may not be used to it either. The first time I had a conversation about this was with a close friend. A mutual friend was in a serious accident. We were on the emotional roller coaster of support because we didn't have experience with situations like this, didn't know what to do, *and* realized we'd never talked about how to support each other during challenging situations.

As the three of us sat together one day during our friend's recovery, we agreed that when everything settled down, we would talk about how to provide friend support when facing tough times, how we wanted to hold each other accountable, and that we would commit to not judging each other if we didn't have capacity to help. When we met, we talked about what we wanted to do for each other, our areas of discomfort, our fears, and who else we could bring in to help if something happened to us. That first conversation was awkward and vulnerable, and we were glad we were having it.

I've had many of these conversations since then. Each one is different because each relationship is different, each person is different, and each situation is different. I've realized that we explore our relationships one experience at a time. Some experiences we have more frequently so we practice and learn more. Some will happen rarely, so we don't have a lot of practice. When I have these conversations, I know I will be surprised by something I learn and I will be a better person for having the conversation.

Step 3: Tips & Tricks to Prevent Becoming Overwhelmed

I choose to care from a place of love.

I have the capacity to thrive every day. When I feel like there is so much going on and I don't know what to do or where to start, when it actually feels like a weight is on me that's holding me down, when I feel responsible for things I know I have no control over, I know I've become overwhelmed and I have no capacity to thrive in my life. It's not where I start or what I intend, it's just thing after thing adding up until I've lost my way.

It is my goal to give care from a place of love and calm. Becoming overwhelmed happens to me when I lose my perspective and my sense of balance about who I am, and what I am best—and not best—qualified to do. If lessons I learn empower me to be present and make the most out of my caregiving experience, being overwhelmed does the opposite.

I'm a very organized person by nature. When I feel overwhelmed, I can't even figure out where to begin organizing. In my work projects, we're always taught to take a big project and keep breaking it down until it is in manageable tasks, and yes, I'm sure you're thinking of one of the many analogies associated with this process! I realized early in my roles of care support that, similar to riding the emotional roller coaster blindfolded, I was trying to break something into manageable tasks blindfolded. I didn't know what I was trying to break down or what a manageable task looked like. Yep, you're right. This added to my feelings of being overwhelmed.

Repackaged Lessons: Become the Observer

For most of her life, my mom struggled with her addiction to alcohol, a complex disease of the brain and body[27]. It's hold on her impacted our family and others around us. It wasn't until many years later I learned that support resources had been available during the period of her struggles. We didn't know what her disease was, so we didn't know what to ask for. At the time, we couldn't help her or us and we were constantly overwhelmed.

My life has been transformed and I have become both a better person and care giver through the practice of learning lessons from my experiences. This practice helps me use my experiences in a positive way and prevent becoming overwhelmed.

This practice involves being the observer of my experiences. There is a significant amount of research available if you want to study "being the observer[28]." The practice was taught to me quite simply, and while it has become immensely valuable in my life, I've kept it as simple as when I first learned it. Being the observer is like being the unemotional third-party, an objective researcher. I observe the experience for the lessons I can gain. I don't judge the experience, I accept it. I don't have to have a purpose for the lessons at the time, I file them away and they'll be available when I have a need for them.

This practice encourages me to stay present in my experiences. I am an objective observer. I don't react unconsciously, project into the future, or apply any number of other "what-if" scenarios that cloud what is actually happening. It creates gifts and blessings from each experience—whether the experience is positive or challenging. This practice gives purpose to that which seems without purpose and, for me, brings the peace that allows me to accept my experiences without either judgment or the need to understand.

This practice became exponentially more valuable to me when I learned that it works both on current experiences as well as ones that occurred in the past. Each experience has valuable lessons. I'm able to repackage lessons from my past to help me with experiences today. Because they're my own experiences, I can relate to them more powerfully and understand the lesson(s) more easily.

The true story below is a very powerful and transformational example of how learning lessons from being the observer helps me positively in my life every day, especially preventing me from becoming overwhelmed.

Clarity Prevents Overwhelm

Because we didn't know what alcoholism was or that it was an addiction, we thought my mom chose to drink. We were thinking rationally about what was going on; we didn't know she couldn't. We didn't understand what she was going through because we saw it from our own understanding. Why would anyone choose to be unhappy? Her behavior was very confusing to us because when she wasn't drinking, she was happy, creative, friendly, and social. When she was drinking, she was unhappy and angry. When she was drinking, she would do the opposite of her sober self; she didn't want to talk with anyone, she wanted to be alone, and she wouldn't create the artwork she loved.

We never knew what to expect. There would be a few days when my mom was in a good place and then, suddenly, she would be in a bad place. We were definitely on an emotional roller coaster blindfolded. We had no idea what caused her sudden changes so we kept trying to figure out what we could do differently to help her. We were constantly on edge, felt helpless and frustrated, and at times felt like our situation was hopeless. We blamed her for what we couldn't do, not realizing she wasn't choosing to behave the way she did.

We were constantly worried about what was coming next. Worry doesn't give us a plan. Worry stops us from thinking clearly and taking positive action. We definitely weren't as helpful as we could have been. We looked at everything my mom did based on how it might trigger her, not staying present in the experience. We lost beautiful memories because we were looking at experiences through our projected fear.

When I learned about being an observer and applied this to past experiences, those experiences now had context and a powerful positive influence in my life. Here are several examples of how objectively observing a situation helps me to prevent feeling overwhelmed as a care giver.

My observation: My mom hadn't chosen her disease. She, and those of us around her, were impacted by the effects of her disease for a long time without knowing what was going on, how to help, or how to feel. Because of this:

- I now have the clarity of compassion for other people's struggles which gives me a heightened sense of awareness and purpose.
- I'm sensitive to others' conflicting emotions because I've been there. I know they may not even realize what they're feeling or that their feelings don't serve them well. I can model how I take actions to help me stay connected with my emotions and how I check in with them to make sure they are serving me.
- I share my stories and model the lessons I've learned from a place of peaceful acceptance and freedom from judgement. My stories and lessons now have the potential to add context to other people's experiences and potentially prevent them from becoming overwhelmed.
- I don't try to fix things that aren't mine to fix. I used to think if I just tried harder, did more, or took on more responsibility, it would make things better. I now know there is a solution, and trying to fix what's not mine to fix is definitely not it.
- I'm an advocate of sharing as many resources as possible with as many people as possible so more time is invested in creating the best experience for both care givers and care receivers. Feeling overwhelmed comes from not knowing what is wrong, what to do, or where to go for help. It doesn't have to be that way and I can be at least one source of information.

My observation: I created my own overwhelmed state when I wasn't present in my mom's alcoholism and when I didn't know what to do. I projected all kinds of incredibly unhealthy things about myself and about our experiences that would snowball into a negative space. I actually made things worse than they were because I kept imagining the worst. This prevented me from the opportunity of seeing what was actually happening. I missed both the beauty in many of my life experiences as well as the opportunity to improve what I could actually control in my life. I now know:

- I only have control over my own actions. Taking an honest inventory of my actions teaches me to take responsibility and informs what I need to do. I now focus on what I have control over to make my experience, and the experience of my care receiver, the best it can be. I don't waste time or emotion on what is not in my control or what is not mine to fix.
- I make myself available to support the people who do have responsibility for things not in my control.
- I don't project experiences into the future. I now live with acceptance, I focus on the present, and I embrace the importance of self-care so I have healthy experiences.
- I don't waste time or emotion on what caused me to become a care giver or my loved one to become a care receiver. Blaming myself, someone, or something else prevents me from experiencing the beneficial feelings, thoughts, emotions, and actions.

Focusing on what I have control over, accepting our experience without judgement, and staying present has eliminated my feelings of being overwhelmed and keeps me emotionally balanced. When something doesn't seem right, I immediately break it down into smaller and smaller tasks until the situation becomes manageable. I begin with what I can control and break it down until I find where I can take action. As I accomplish each tiny task, I am better prepared. I then gain clarity on how to accomplish the bigger tasks.

Don't get me wrong, there are still times when I'm not sure what to do. One thing I do know is that others are going through what I'm going through. I'm not alone and I can both talk things out with others and find resources to help.

Choose Your Perspective, Choose Your Experience

I've been fascinated with perspective since the fourth grade, when I had my first experience with the exciting potential of it in my life. Our Language Arts teacher gave our entire class the first half of a story and asked each of us to write its ending. I immediately thought of an ending, wrote it, and was eager to share it when our teacher asked. She didn't call on me first and I was so disappointed that initially, I wasn't actively listening to another student as he shared his story ending. However, something he said did catch my attention. His ending was really good and it was an idea that hadn't occurred to me! When the next student shared, I was keen to listen, and again, the ending was both good and an idea I hadn't even considered. I finally shared my story ending which was different from the other two. I was still proud of it and by that time, I was more curious about how others imagined the ending rather than fixating on my own creativity.

Over the years, I've continued to learn from this experience. I've found that being open to many perspectives is a powerful tool for not becoming overwhelmed. I'm naturally wired to focus being part of the solution and making each experience as positive as I can for myself and others. I know people sometimes focus on what could go wrong, see the negative, and expect a negative outcome. I have learned valuable lessons from their perspective. There is a wide range of perspectives in between that have validity.

I embrace other perspectives to inform how I think, act, and feel, or how I don't want to think, act, and feel. Then I develop my own perspective as my lens through which I see my experiences. I don't let someone else's definition automatically become mine.

One example occurred during a meeting with a psychiatrist, an expert who has many years' experience working with patients. She began our first session by saying, quite emotionally, that dementia is a horrible, dreadful, awful, debilitating disease and she was sorry we had to suffer through it (I was so shocked at her description that I committed her words to memory and I wrote them down). She is a person of authority, so I could have chosen to embrace her perspective as my own. However, seeing our journey through that lens overwhelmed me.

I chose to respect her perspective. Instead of taking it as my own, I used my discomfort with her perspective to inform how I created the lens of my perspective. Her lens is her authentic view and that doesn't mean it has to be mine. Just because she is considered an expert doesn't make her perspective right for me. The perspective I developed, that serves me today, is honoring how serious the disease is while also seeking to experience the person. I'm able to see and enjoy the beauty in the tiniest of signs while remaining present to changes in the disease that merit responsible action.

In the memory care unit where my husband, Jack, lives, musicians frequently come in to play songs that stimulate residents' memories. Families and care givers are also there, and we all enjoy seeing how much the music positively touches each resident. For one resident (Amanda), her disease has progressed to a point where she has minimal ability to move her hands and feet. One day, a musician who came in played quite energetic songs, and most of us were singing and/or moving along with the music. I looked down and saw Amanda's foot tapping ever so slightly. I shared this with everyone in our group and we were all so excited—one would think we'd just won the lottery. We chose to focus on the beauty of this tiny movement and have a positive experience rather than focus on her inabilities. I get to choose the perspective that serves me— so does everyone.

Be With Community So Community Can Be With You

I'm part of communities in multiple areas of my life. My community members help and support me and give me the opportunity to help and support them. When I have capacity to lean in and help, I do. When I need help, community members are there for me. It's part of why I'm not overwhelmed. I know I'll never be alone and someone I know has wisdom that will help me with what I don't know or can't see.

I can imagine what my caregiving experience would look like without community because for many years, I wasn't part of one that focused on supporting care givers. My experience alone was so much more challenging and I was overwhelmed. I had to learn each lesson on my own. I didn't know there were alternatives. I couldn't benefit from the experiences of others or receive their support.

Once I joined a community of care givers, every part of my experience became more manageable and ultimately, better. It's not that my care receiver's condition improved. I improved. My mindset, attitude and timely access to resources improved. It was an incredibly positive change in such a short time.

When I didn't have my community, I became accustomed to handling things on my own. "I can do this" was my constant mantra. (I sound like Bob from my first caregiving experience!) I thought that if I asked for help, it would be a sign of weakness, or a sign I couldn't handle things. Please, I beg you, if this is your thinking as well, may I invite you to consider a different perspective? Accepting help and joining a support community!

Being part of a community makes me stronger, more confident, and more capable. Because I'm not trying to figure out everything on my own, I'm not overwhelmed and I feel better. Because I feel better, I have the capacity to lean in and help others. When I help others, I feel better. When my emotional roller coaster ride takes me on another sudden turn or drop, I don't feel like I'm falling uncontrollably; I know people are there with whom I can talk, and gain support and ideas.

Community members have our backs. Sometimes we don't know what to look for in ourselves, sometimes we can't see what's there. The common foundation of our community means we're not strangers, we just don't know each other yet, and we have something in common. We're able to naturally be more open and candid, our community creates an invitation for us to lean in and care for each other.

Have you ever been so close to a situation that you couldn't recognize it? Someone else, someone who cared for you and had a more objective view could see it more clearly. When they shared their perspective with you, things became so obvious you wondered how you missed it. Community can play that role.

Compassion Fatigue

One very important example of a myopic viewpoint is a disorder known as *compassion fatigue*. A good thing—compassion, out of balance—fatigue. Compassion fatigue can develop from a place of love. One explanation identifies it as caregivers focusing on others without practicing self-care. They lose self-awareness and don't realize they are developing destructive behaviors, including apathy and isolation. They may not be able to contain bottled up emotions. As a result, they may turn to substance abuse to treat the symptoms of this secondary traumatic stress disorder[29].

Communities of care supporters know the signs and symptoms of compassion fatigue, burnout, and exhaustion. I've been part of meetings where we've helped someone see the changes in their behavior that have resulted in being out of balance. We've also helped them know they are in a safe place to explore and address them.

If you participate in a community that doesn't fit you, I encourage you not to give up. Please consider trying different groups until you find the one that feels comfortable. I found there wasn't a formula for the right fit; it was more of a sense I felt when I was in the group. I didn't fit in with some groups. I found groups I looked forward to participating with and learning from.

One of the best tips I've learned, and has worked every time, came from one of our support meetings. In "Step 2: I Don't Know What I Don't Know," in the section titled

"Definitions Clarify, Labels Mislead," I mentioned the first part of this tip about the definition of "home." Here's the second part. This came about because Jack was starting to get confused in the evening and thought he had to go home, even though we were at home. I had tried several things, and nothing was working. I was concerned because Jack was adamant about going home.

Someone in our group shared a very helpful redirection tip. When her husband began making a similar request, she would say, "Ok, let's go. Oh, may we please stop at Walmart on the way so I can pick something up?" Her husband would always agree, so they would go to Walmart (she picked Walmart because they are open 24 hours), look around for a while then drive back to their home. By this time her care receiver had forgotten about wanting to go to a different "home" than theirs and was fine going back to their home.

I had the opportunity to try this same strategy that very evening. It kept Jack calm and the distraction reset him so he was ready to come home. It would not have occurred to me and it worked every time!

Memory Care Community

When my mother-in-love, Donna, moved my dad into a memory care facility, she modeled the importance and value of becoming an active participant in their memory care community. Thanks to the lessons I learned from Donna and others in our caregiving support community, I am an active participant in the memory care community where Jack now lives. My goal for him is to be safe and live in an environment that provides his best opportunities for happiness. I believe my participation in the memory care community is extremely important to achieve this goal. Please know I'm not saying my way is the right way—it's the way that works for me and it's based on tips and tricks that were shared with me.

One way I achieve my goal for him is to make sure he is the best resident he can be and I am the best care supporter I can be. This means I do whatever I can to facilitate his role as a good resident and assist those who provide him care. In any of my roles of care support, I begin by observing Jack in his activities at different times of day.

In my role of Primary Caregiver, several of the things I do are:

- Make sure Jack has the right clothing and toiletries.
- Observe him standing up and sitting down, walking, toileting, eating, drinking, brushing his teeth, socializing. What is easy? Does he pick up his feet when he is walking or is he shuffling? How easy is it for him to eat different types of food? What can I be doing to make sure it is as easy for him to get through his day as possible?
- Participate on our memory care family council. We meet every other month to talk about any care provision issues and also recognize what's positive. We are the voice for our care receivers; each of us have different perspectives and experiences so it's important we gather information from everyone. This helps us have our best understanding and the management team is informed of our concerns in maintaining their current level of operational support.
- Maintain an open line of communication with the business team so I can ask questions and be supportive.

In the role of Care Partner, several of the things I do are:

- Work regularly with the medical care team to understand what they are observing, if he needs medical and/or behavioral support, and then work together to find the best solution.
- Be sensitive to his other care partners requirements in providing support and find ways to improve Jack's experience while reducing his care partners' extraneous support. Several examples of this include:
    - o Jack began having difficulty remembering how to sit in a chair as well as on the toilet. It started taking him anywhere from a couple of minutes to more than ten minutes. He is assisted by a care partner the entire time. Although they didn't complain about the amount of time it took, I noticed this change in Jack and how sitting was challenging. Together, his care partners and I found modifications that make it easier for him to sit. Now, sitting down takes much less time, which frees up his care partners while still providing Jack a positive experience. By asking questions of his care team and members of the caregiving community, I learned there was a solution that was helpful for everyone.
    - o Jack is sometimes resistant to brushing his teeth and shaving. I shared with his nursing assistants what I did to get him to do these daily tasks. There are different care providers, so it became impractical for me to tell each of them separately. I wrote a sign, laminated it, and put it on the wall of his bathroom. Sometimes he still resists shaving, and he does brush his teeth twice a day!

We Are "Framily"

I learned a term I wish I had created and am glad someone did. "Framily" is the term for friends who are like family. I am a proud member of our memory care community "framily." We pitch in to help whenever and wherever we can.

Compassionate Truth, Compassionate Lies

This isn't about the right way or the wrong way to talk with our care receiver. It's about multiple perspectives when participating in an experience. My personal preference is telling the truth. I grew up with very strong consequences for telling lies; we just didn't lie, and I feel uncomfortable lying. Do I tell lies? Yes, I sometimes do. I don't feel good about them and my body language gives me away. I'm not going to ask you to change your position on lying vs. telling the truth, I'm sharing how my perspective helps me stay more emotionally balanced and prevent becoming overwhelmed.

It wasn't until I joined my care support community that I was introduced to the concept of compassionate lies. It was explained as telling a lie to our care receiver that helps them stay in their routine and stay calm. While the concept makes a lot of sense and works, the perspective I chose to develop is that I am telling my care receiver the truth which helps them feel their best. I realize it's a minor distinction, and for me, it's a very important one. The difference is in my intent, delivery, and impact.

I've observed that when I tell my care receiver the most helpful truth, they feel good and so do I. My grandmother stopped remembering I was her granddaughter. She was always happy to see me and thought I was a friend of the family. The first few times, we explained to her I was her granddaughter. Several times, she told us we were wrong and became agitated. One time, she apologized and I could tell she felt bad. We realized that in her mind, I wasn't her granddaughter. Her heart remembered I was someone she liked and was happy to see. I was fine with being a friend of the family because it supported her happiness.

By stepping into her truth, we allowed her to maintain the dignity of her experience and enjoy welcoming me happily. One of the great phrases used in the communities of those who have a loved one with a type of dementia is:

"What the mind can't remember, the heart never forgets."

As Jack transitioned away from carrying a wallet, he'd sometimes stop all of a sudden in a panic that he'd forgotten it. I'd look him in the eyes, smile, explain in a positive and reassuring manner that he put it safely away in his drawer, and we could go get it if he wanted. He would calm down right away and quit thinking about it. Did the real truth serve a purpose here? What was different for me if I told him a compassionate lie or compassionate truth? If I'm telling a compassionate lie, I'm trying to avoid something unnecessarily difficult and it shows in my body language and eyes. When I'm telling a compassionate truth, I'm honestly trying to do the best thing for both him and me.

One of the best examples of quick-thinking compassionate truth is when Jack and I were dining together in his memory care unit. One of the support team members who helps with dining was picking up Jack's plate. He reached for his wallet and couldn't find it. He went into a panic because he wanted to leave her a tip. She gave him a big smile and told him he'd already given her one. She told him he'd said it was so important to him to give her a tip that he'd given it to her during the meal and she really appreciated it. She was positive and supportive and helped him feel great instead of feeling frustrated.

I like telling the truth that makes my care receiver feel good. It makes me feel good, too.

Our Journey is Part of Everyone's Journey—I Invite You to Invite Them In

I continue to see that people either completely agree or completely disagree with the perspective I'm about to share. What I've learned in my caregiving experiences, is having everyone aware of our diagnoses helps my care receivers and me prevent overwhelm. This being said, I do respect those who choose to keep their journey private.

When I'm in caregiving support meetings, I hear loved ones share what they're doing to keep family and friends from knowing what's going on. Sometimes it's the care receiver who doesn't want anyone to know, sometimes it's the care giver, sometimes it's both of them. The care givers talk about how physically, mentally and emotionally exhausting their journey becomes. Not only are they providing the majority of care for their loved one and going through their own emotional roller coaster, they're juggling the different stories they are telling friends and family. This seems like a recipe for overwhelm. Even though I respect their choice, I can't imagine how this is sustainable.

When we share our diagnosis with others, we also accept their capacity to continue with us on the journey. For some people, we know our news ignites their compassion and desire to help, and they do. For others, it raises memories of previous experiences and they aren't comfortable going back down that path. We understand and accept their choice. We make sure they know this and that it doesn't change how we feel about them. Still others are uncomfortable seeing the changes in their loved ones and can't be around them anymore. Again, we have the opportunity to share that we accept their choice and that it doesn't change how we feel about them.

Many years ago, I learned the phrase "Some people come into our lives for a reason, some come into our lives for a season, and some come into our lives for a lifetime." This phrase is a perfect example of people who are put into situations that teach them insights about themselves. Their experiences help them decide whether they have capacity to stay with us on our journey, step away temporarily, or step away permanently.

No matter someone else's capacity to participate in our journey, we accept them exactly the way they are. We aren't investing any energy or emotion in lying to them or being upset if they don't have the capacity to journey with us. This helps eliminate any negative feelings or feelings of overwhelm in our relationships with them.

And When They Do, Let Them Help!

I find caregiving support meetings are like doing a Google search with live people. Ask a question, a variety of responses are instantly returned. One example of this is: *How do we invite service personnel to understand and support us?* During one of our meetings, someone talked about how uncomfortable it was in restaurants when servers got frustrated at the care receiver's struggle to order. Our meeting hosts showed us business cards they printed. I had used these cards successfully several times and decided I wanted to have our own made with my dad's name on them. When Jack was diagnosed, we did the same for him. When we went to a restaurant, or somewhere else with service personnel, I would hand the card to them. They were invited to consider treating us with compassion rather than frustration.

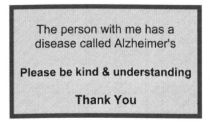 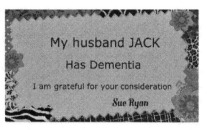

On several occasions, the server didn't read the card right away and became frustrated when my dad or Jack struggled with their order. When the server returned after having read the card, their entire demeanor was positive. They understood the reason behind the behavior.

Golf as a Team Sport

Sometimes letting people help is a team effort. Friends of ours (I'll use the names Debbie and Joe), recently received the diagnosis of Alzheimer's disease for Joe. Joe loves to play golf and participated in a league. As his disease progressed, it was harder for his team to have him play with them because it was increasingly harder for him to remember how to play and keep score. Many of the gentlemen in the league have known each other for many years—some are college fraternity brothers. Thankfully, what began as a frustrating experience for everyone turned into a beautiful experience.

Debbie and Joe's friends wanted Joe to continue playing the game he loves. He's a very social person and enjoys time with his friends; on the days he was playing golf, he would be ready hours before it was time to leave. Debbie wanted him to remain connected to something he could still do and that he still loved. She could use the time he was on the golf course for self-care and errands. Debbie, and several of the league members, worked together and came up with a solution. Joe would no longer play in the league and several of his friends would play golf with him and have lunch together on a different day. Everyone was happy and, on one of the days, Joe hit a hole-in-one!

A Walk to the Mailbox

My dad had always been very routine-oriented. One of the early signs something was wrong was the challenges he began having with his routines. My parents lived in a community with a common location for all mailboxes. Every day at the same time, my dad would walk from their home to the community post office, pick up the mail and walk back home. He began forgetting to pick up the mail, forgetting the location of the post office and the location of their mailbox, even though the community post office was visible from their home. Donna shared with neighbors and the community staff that my dad was having issues and they became concerned about both my dad and Donna. She would prompt my dad to go to the post office for the mail and make sure he got started in the right direction. Neighbors would "appear" part way along his journey and visit with him, actually walking with him until he arrived at the mail area. A staff member just happened to be in the area of the mailboxes and would casually help my dad get his mail.

This helped my dad continue having a sense of purpose and helped Donna give him things to do to keep him active. It also gave their neighbors and the community staff a sense of purpose. They didn't have to help, they wanted to. They felt good about being able to help. Donna had peace of mind, she didn't have to be concerned about my dad's safety.

Jack's Invisible Helpers

Jack was an active member of a large men's group. When he stopped driving, either one of his friends or I would take him to their meeting so he could continue attending. It was a great social time for him and a time for me to run errands. His friends told me they would keep an eye on him. One of his friends told me they had put a discreet system in place for Jack's safety that ensured he wouldn't accidentally leave the building. One evening, I finished my errands early and was waiting in the front hall. I saw Jack get up to go to the restroom and I watched as his friends put their "system" into action. I was so grateful, I nearly burst into tears. A gentleman near the front door casually stood up and went to stand near the front door in case Jack decided to leave. Another went near the coffee because Jack liked getting a cup of coffee on his way back from the restroom. He poured two cups of coffee and offered Jack one, so it didn't seem like it was just for Jack. They could have seen Jack as a distraction that took them away from their meeting. Instead, they saw it as an opportunity to show kindness to both Jack and me. I had emotional peace-of-mind in knowing Jack was safe and happy. I was incredibly grateful for their thoughtfulness and it definitely prevented overwhelm.

Until Jack moved into memory care, he chose to attend catholic mass every day. We planned our activities around this so he could go to mass wherever we were. When Jack stopped driving, I chose to stop going to the gym in the morning so he could still attend church every day. In our church, we were surrounded by people who also attended church daily. One day, a gentleman who I didn't know well, came over to us after church and explained that he drove right past our subdivision on his way to and from church. He offered to bring Jack home after church. From that day on until Jack moved into memory care, this gentleman brought Jack home and I got to go to the gym. He would periodically tell me about wonderful conversations he and Jack had during the drive home. This gesture of generous kindness helped all of us.

I could have turned down offers from others for help because I didn't want to impose on anyone and because I felt like I should be able to do everything myself. That's the way I used to feel. I then repackaged a transforming lesson from years before. This lesson allows me to let others help because it makes them feel good.

Supporting Despite Our Protests

I was in my mid-thirties when my mom passed away. I was right in the middle of my sales career, a time when I was proving I could handle everything that came my way. I was living in Chicago, Illinois. My mom passed away in Florida, the funeral and cemetery in which she was being buried were in Iowa. I was navigating the arrangements in all three locations. One of my most treasured friends, Ann, who also lived in Chicago, called to ask what she could do to help and to tell me she was coming to the funeral.

I'm sure you know what I told her, "Thank you. I appreciate your offer very much. I know you're busy. You stay there, I'll be fine." We hung up the phone and off I went to continue "handling" everything. During my mom's funeral, when it became time for me to give her eulogy, I walked up to the front of the church, took a deep breath, climbed the steps to the pulpit, turned around and looked at the congregation before I began speaking. There, in the middle of the church, was Ann. I promise you, seeing her at that moment and knowing she drove more than four hours that morning because she wanted to, is one of the most transformational experiences of my life.

Ann hadn't asked to help out of a sense of obligation. Ann knew I was capable of handling everything. She knew I would find a way to get everything done. Ann drove over that morning to be with our family because it was important to *her*, because it was what *she* wanted to do. From that day forward, when someone offers to help, I say "thank you." I invite them into our experience based on their capacity to participate and I am incredibly grateful. It's freeing to allow someone to do something kind for you. If you want to know a sure-fire way to reduce overwhelm, consider allowing others to help in any way they can, even when you *can* "handle" it.

I have learned it's helpful to be specific both when I'm offering to help someone and when others want to know how they can help. It helps me be specific about the capacity I have available to help others and it makes it easier for others to know what kinds of support I need that fit their capacity to help. These can both change frequently.

Just as I have different capacities to help at different times, when people offer to help us, I respect that they have different capacities. Have you ever gone into a store where they have gift suggestions and price ranges? This helps people find gifts that fit whatever price range they can afford. I created something similar with care support. I make lists with the types of support that are helpful and modify them periodically. These options for them to consider are based on different amounts of time or effort involved. It's very easy to do. I will perhaps share three different types of help, making it easy for them to pick based on the amount of time and/or effort involved.

For example, on my list may be taking Jack to his men's meeting, taking him for lunch, or picking up something for me at the grocery store. I do the same thing when I am offering support. Rather than just ask if I can do anything for them, which doesn't help them know what I have capacity for, I may tell them I can bring them dinner on a specific night, go to the airport to pick up people who are coming to town, or sit with them at the hospital. Sometimes they don't need what I'm offering. Knowing the type of capacity I have to provide support, and knowing I'm there for them, makes it easier for them to ask me for the specific help they do need.

Accepting help from others as a way to diminish overwhelm reminded me of an exercise I did as a Girl Scout. It was a clear lesson about both the importance and value of working together. Since I connected it with accepting help from others, it has taken on an even more valuable meaning as a way to prevent overwhelm, and support others who want to help. It prepares either me to help provide, or prepares others provide me, much appreciated support.

Our Girl Scout troop members were divided into groups. We were told our exercise was to teach us about strength and flexibility. (The real object was for us to learn how much stronger and more flexible we are when we work together.) Each group received four pieces of string. We were asked to tie one piece of string to a weighted box and then slide the box off the edge of our counter. We did that and the string broke. It wasn't strong enough to hold the box. We then braided the other three pieces of string together creating a rope of four strings. We tied this rope to the box and dropped it again. The rope held. We did several other tests with more weight and the braided rope continued to hold.

We saw the obvious, the braided string stretched, and it continued to support the box, while the single string didn't. We were then taught the real lessons of our experiment. We learned each string is vitally important, and not always strong enough on its own. The rope of four strings was both stronger and more flexible than the single string because it was braided together. We learned that when we work together, we are made stronger because all of our ideas come together. We learned we are more flexible because when we bring together several ideas, we create something we couldn't have created on our own. We learned that multiple perspectives help us consider more possibilities.

Yes, it was a simple exercise, yet it has remained a clear demonstration of the importance of working together so we have more choices. These lead to better outcomes and less overwhelm.

I Won't Always Have Capacity

I have learned to accept that there are periods of time (I call them "seasons") when I don't have capacity to support others. I used to feel bad if I couldn't give back to others for what they did for me. I would try to help; I'd feel overwhelmed because I felt like I wasn't doing enough, and I wasn't getting done what I needed to do. Of course, I didn't share my feelings with anyone because I didn't want to seem like I was making excuses, and I didn't want others to feel bad. It truly weighed me down. Funny enough, I didn't feel that way about others' actions and I expected something different from myself!

I've now learned others don't expect that of me. I no longer feel bad or overwhelmed when I am in a season without capacity to help others as much as I want to. When others don't have capacity to help me, I accept it and understand. Just as I know those around me will help when they can, they know I will gladly help when I can. When people want to help me, I find ways they can. No help is too little. All kindness generates gratitude, and gratitude generates joy. I prefer joy over overwhelm.

Yes You Can - You've Done This Before!

This is one of those lessons I didn't learn in my early roles of care support; it's based on a practice I learned originally in my professional career and now use in all areas of my life. If I had used it sooner as a care giver, I feel sure our lives and our experiences would have been better. It is a much healthier and more balanced approach to managing the responsibilities involved with care giving. For me, the most valuable part of incorporating this practice is how practical it is. It makes sense and it helps me evaluate, in each role of care support, who the best resource is to provide care.

I believe most of us have been part of something that began with just us. As it began to grow, we needed additional people to provide us expertise and/or capacity we didn't have, so whatever we were working on would be successful. This may have been building our business, working on a school project, organizing a charity event, running a church bazaar, planning a family vacation, and/or creating a home project. The examples are endless.

Creating the most positive care giving experience is exactly the same.

At the beginning of my role in care support for my husband, Jack, I was able to handle everything on my own. While Jack and I didn't formally create goals for our experience with his diagnosis of a type of Dementia, I created my goals for our experience based on our conversations:

- Keep Jack safe and create the environment that supports him being happy.
- Make our journey as positive as possible for each of us and those who support us.

In business, we were taught to always focus on the highest and best use of our time and expertise so we could make our most positive impact. We surround ourselves with others who support us through the highest and best use of their time and expertise, so we collectively make our most positive impact. As it became important for me to take responsibility for more tasks Jack had been doing, there came a point when I didn't have the time capacity to accomplish everything that needed to be done. As our journey continued, I didn't have the expertise to know how to keep Jack safe and create the environment that supported him being happy - I needed expertise from others!

Implementing what I had used in my professional career, I began by identifying what the highest and best use of my time was, so I had clarity on what I could take responsibility for and where I needed support. I began adding people to our team who supported both Jack and me with the help they provided. For example, our church had volunteers who came to our home and would share time with our care receiver for up to two hours. This was helpful because I could get through my list of errands more quickly. Next, I added someone who could help with transportation for Jack to activities that were very important to him and supported his happiness.

During one of the times I spoke about this in a care giving support meeting, someone in our group said they couldn't afford help. They didn't have anyone to help them and they had no family around. They said this could only work for people with money. I absolutely respect their perspective. There are significant opportunities for us to provide additional complementary, subsidized, and low-cost resources for respite care and care giving support (please see Making the Experience Bigger Than Me beginning on page 165?). I researched and learned there are many organizations, faith based, government, community, non-profit, and individual, who provide complementary, low-cost, and sometimes subsidized support.

While I do pay for some of the resources that support Jack's and my care, many of the resources I benefit from are people who volunteer to help because it means so much to them to have an opportunity to do something of value and purpose, the highest and best use of their time. Often, these are people who benefitted from others leaning in to support them during their time of need; these are mutual gifts.

In the experience I just shared, one of the magical moments of care giving support occurred. Individuals in the room leaned in to share what they'd learned, resources they used, people who had been helpful to them. Several offered their time. What started out as a comment out of frustration, turned into an opportunity for others to share their experiences, provide support and hope, and give this person strength in their journey through knowing there was help available and they weren't alone.

The highest and best use of my time, and the resources to support achieving our goals through time and/or expertise, continue to change. I frequently evaluate each area, so I am doing my best and have the best resources to support our creating the most positive impact. Each area of expertise I learn from helps me be a better care giver. Each individual who invests their time and expertise to help keep Jack safe and create the environment that supports his happiness, makes a positive impact. The commitment and support of others strengthens me and adds to my passion to help others, so they experience how powerfully and positively it touches our lives.

Self-Care! Don't Be Humpty Dumpty

It was easy for me to "shave pieces of myself away" to care for my loved ones; I was giving care from a place of love. It was modeled to me multiple times that, with our spouse, this is part of our "for better or for worse" agreement. For many years, I also believed I should handle it all. As my care receiver's needs continued to increase, I looked at where I could find the capacity to take on more and "shave off" something from my own activities. I did this again and again, and I kept on doing it. I thought this was what I was supposed to do. There finally came a time when I didn't have any more to "shave off".

I've read a variety of reports showing statistics about caregivers dying before their care receiver. The stories are very sad. I've found the results of the studies to validate the concern to be inconsistent with the numbers they report, so I'm not going to share them. What I took away is how important it is for me not to become one of their future statistics, and to help everyone else do the same. My vision is that everyone in roles of care support learns how to thrive on their journeys and feel great about themselves, so we make our most positive impact.

Leaders of our care support groups frequently talk about the importance of self-care and give us examples of things we can do in this area[30]. When there just wasn't anything else I could "shave off," I looked at the list and began trying some of them. Each time I did, I felt awkward, I felt uncomfortable, and I felt like I should be doing something for my care receiver. I'm not sure what caused it, but all of a sudden, a lightbulb went off for me. I realized many of the things I had willingly stopped doing were actually very helpful forms of self-care; I just hadn't been thinking about them in that way.

I've come to learn that many of us, in our lives outside giving care, don't do a good job modeling self-care either. I was one of those people. I've learned if I don't make myself a priority, I can't care effectively for anyone else. My care receiver and I are on our journey together. I want to be strong for that person, especially when they can't be strong for themselves. It's very simple; I'm responsible for taking care of myself, so I take care of myself responsibly.

Have you quit going to the doctor because of how much time it takes and how difficult it is to make sure your care receiver is ok while you're away? I did. When two of my friends, within a few months of each other, told me they had been diagnosed with breast cancer, I realized I couldn't remember the last time I'd been to the doctor.

I have learned to be conscious and intentional when I "shave off" something, so it doesn't end up being my life. While I may choose to do something different for a season in my life, that benefits my care receiver, I make sure I am not shaving off something that may have long-term negative impacts on my health. When it's something significant, I also reach out to someone else to talk it through with them so I gain valuable insights and potential options I may not have considered.

All the king's horses and all the king's men couldn't put Humpty Dumpty back together again. I want to keep myself together for my care receiver *and* for me.

Step 4: Dealing With The Every Day

I will never be alone.
Help and care are all around me. I receive so I can give.

When I was taught the importance of focusing on my life today, it transformed my life in several positive ways. I now stay in the present. I don't waste time or emotion focusing on what I can't control. I don't cloud the potential of my day by projecting what might—or might not be—in the future. This doesn't mean I don't research, learn, plan, or prepare. It means I focus on what actually is happening and, based on that, I call on my experiences and support resources to give me ideas of what to do. It means I look at what I am responsible for and what I actually have control over.

Another incredibly valuable lesson I've learned in my life is that the only thing I actually have control over is me! The more I try to control other people or things, the less I am able to focus on what actually is happening and make wise choices. I am much calmer and more peaceful because I'm not overwhelmed by the magnitude of my situation.

I used to look at every experience in our journey as something charged with emotion. I've learned it doesn't have to be that way. I now know how to keep experiences in perspective so they don't generate overwhelm or take me out of balance. In order for this to happen, I must be intentional about how I choose to feel about my experiences. If I'm not, I can quickly lose myself.

What The Mind Can't Remember, The Heart Never Forgets

A friend of mine sent me a t-shirt with the slogan on it, "What the Mind Can't Remember, The Heart Never Forgets." As the disease or condition of my care receiver continues to progress, they move farther and farther away from what has been healthy and normal for them. For example, as the disease of Alzheimer's progresses with my husband Jack, he is gradually losing access to his memories. I accept that completely so I stay present to his current capabilities and meet him where he's at. What I also do every day is make sure I implant memories into his heart.

For most of my life, when my dad kissed me goodnight, said goodbye, or when we were ending our phone calls, I said the exact same thing back to him. As his disease progressed, his mind quit remembering who I was when he saw me, as I knew it would. Each time I saw him, I got close to him, looked him right in the eyes, got a big smile on my face and told him: "I love you more than life its very own self." His face always lit up.

Dr. Paul Pearsall was a licensed clinical neuropsychologist, clinical professor at the University of Hawai`i, and on the Board of Directors of the Hawai`i State Consortium for Integrative

Health Care. He was a member of the heart transplant study team at the University of Arizona School of Medicine, and a Senior Research Advisor for the Human Energy Systems Laboratory at the University of Arizona. His ground-breaking research on heart transplant recipients receiving the memories of their donors led to the formation of the Cleveland Clinic's new Heart/Mind program[31]. There have been many articles and research papers written about the phenomenon of heart transplant patients taking on personality traits, preferences, and memories of their donors[32]. In his 1998 book, *The Heart's Code*[33], Dr. Pearsall provides information deeply grounded in research about the background of this phenomenon along with powerful, substantiated stories.

What I took away from studying his work is that even if my care receiver has the diagnosis of a type of dementia and their "head brain" struggles with its memories, their "heart brain" remembers.

From the day Jack was diagnosed, I continue to greet him the exact same way every time I see him. His disease has progressed to where he remembers who I am less and less. When I see him, I get close to him, look him right in the eyes, get a big smile on my face and say to him: "Hello, love of my life. How's the man of my dreams?" His face always lights up. There may be a day when he is not able to express that he remembers, and the heart never forgets.

This lesson has become more powerful for me in the broader context of how I am with everyone, and it's a valuable resource I use to help me stay present and focused on others. With every action I take, I have the opportunity to imprint positively in someone's life. I see this as a gift I'm receiving as part of my caregiving journey and being committed to learning how to provide the best experience for my care receiver.

First, Don't Lose Yourself. Second, It Can Happen Almost Instantly

These are two lessons I've learned about dealing with the everyday which are related to each other. I thought the first one was powerful; I had no idea the second part was waiting for me to make sure I got the point!

My mom passed away quite unexpectedly. It was right before I moved into a home I'd purchased. My mom and I had talked excitedly day after day about where I would put the furniture, how I would decorate, and where I could plant a garden. My mom was an incredibly gifted artist and gardener. It was as though she could visualize my home and yard better than I could. She had wonderful ideas about what to do and was looking forward to coming to visit to help decorate my new home and plant our garden.

When I returned home from her funeral, I began working on my home, putting in place the things she had visualized. It was, perhaps, a way of my working through my grief, although I didn't recognize it as the grieving process. I worked on my home and garden first thing in the morning before going to work. I worked on it when I got home in the evening. I began to turn down opportunities to get together with friends so I could work on my home. I was at one home and garden center or another when they opened in the morning and sometimes just before they closed at night. As soon as I completed one thing, I began another. Sometimes I would work on a project in one room, walk through another room to get a tool, spot something in the room I was in and start to work on it.

One evening, I walked into my kitchen and felt faint. That was completely out of the ordinary for me. I sat down and tried to figure out what had caused it. I realized I hadn't eaten all day, something else completely out of the ordinary for me! What came to me in that moment was that I had lost myself in working on my home. I had been working on it night and day, and when I was away from my home, I felt like I should be there working on it. I was consumed by it.

That wasn't where I had started. If someone had said to me, "Why don't you work on your home as many hours as you can, day and night?" I would have laughed at them and replied, "No way!" I learned that losing myself wasn't something intentional. Losing myself had happened gradually because I lost focus, boundaries and balance.

I hadn't identified what would be practical to do in a day. How would I know I had completed it? How did I want to feel when I accomplished it? I took a step back, made a list of all of the outstanding projects and scheduled them, one day at a time. I also added other items in my calendar like dinner with friends, exercise, and church. I found my way back to myself by remembering what was important to me.

How does this relate to dealing with every day in my caregiving journey? I thought I had learned my lesson about losing myself when I was working on my house. I had become very intentional about staying in the moment and focusing on the day, until Hurricane Irma in 2017. The details of what occurred aren't as important as the lesson.

The route for Hurricane Irma was projected to directly hit our town, to literally come up the street where we live. When I made the decision to evacuate us before the hurricane, I almost immediately lost myself in caring for Jack. I was completely focused on his safety and reducing his anxiety, and I didn't realize it for several weeks. I wasn't taking care of myself. I was literally with him, and focused on him, twenty-four hours a day.

It's not enough for me to practice staying in the moment. I need to be aware of and prepared for what can trigger me to lose myself. I learned that the shift can happen almost instantly. For me, it was a significant event. I am now aware of this and I know what I need to do the next time I experience my trigger, a significant event. I now practice massive acceptance and radical presence. In Step 5, Finding Hope, I share exactly how I do this and why it works for me.

Have you ever lost yourself caring for someone? Do you know what you need to do to prevent it from happening in the future? It's definitely worth figuring out.

They Do In The Moment

It used to surprise me when my care receivers couldn't remember something mere seconds after it had occurred. They would ask when they were going to eat, and their empty plate was still in front of them from their meal. They would get ready to take the dog out when they had been out less than five minutes earlier. They would ask the same question even as I finished answering it. I now fully accept this.

Learning about my care receiver's diagnosis gives me the opportunity to develop my perspective from a place of acceptance. Combining this with staying fully present in each moment, I now focus even more intentionally on making each event as rich as possible for my care receiver and for myself. I've also expanded this approach to the rest of my life. The moments I experience, and those in which I participate for others, keep getting better and better.

I fully respect how very hard it is for people to grasp the significant changes in their loved ones, especially if they are not with them on a daily basis. Not all moments are obvious moments of joy! There are plenty of very challenging times. There are also moments where there is calm, quiet, and peace. Either way, when I practice massive acceptance and radical presence (more about this in Step 5), I see the positive effect on my care receiver's actions, emotions, face, expression, and body language. These add to their communication and help me meet them where they're at so I can better support them.

With some types of neurocognitive disorders, short-term memory—also known as active memory—is significantly diminished as the disease progresses[34]. Simply stated, experiences of the moment don't stay in a person's memory so they can recall them. I used to confuse this with thinking the experiences themselves didn't matter to the person. I've learned that they still have the experience and, in the moment, it still matters to them. The joy is beautiful to observe, the sadness is unfiltered. The pleasure and the pain are both very real.

While the experience may be gone quickly, it doesn't diminish the moment. It's like savoring an incredibly rich and delicious chocolate; I enjoy it in the moment and the flavor does go away quickly. This doesn't mean I don't enjoy that chocolate to its fullest while I'm eating it!

In "Step 3: Tips and Tricks to Prevent Becoming Overwhelmed," I mentioned Amanda, tapping her foot ever so slightly to the music. In that moment, she was filled with joy and expressed it in the way she could. My husband, Jack, loves music. The musicians learn which songs residents like and play those songs every time they play for the residents. When they sing "Take Me Out to the Ball Game," Jack sings out loud with a huge smile on his face. When they sing the sad Irish ballad "Danny Boy," my 100% Irish husband sings out loud, too, shoulders shaking from his sobs.

One of our friends mentioned he quit visiting Jack because he didn't think Jack knew who he was anymore. He said he knew Jack wouldn't remember he had called moments after it ended, so he didn't call anymore, either. I agreed with him that Jack didn't remember who he was, and that he most likely wouldn't remember he had called. I explained to him how much the moment itself meant to Jack, even if it didn't last, and if he ever wanted to call because it was what *he* wanted to, it would be fine. I also reassured him that I completely accepted and understood his decision. I want everyone to do only what is comfortable for them.

I learned a valuable lesson when the sister of a friend was seriously ill in the hospital. My friend had gone to see her sister in intensive care and my friend couldn't recognize her sister. My friend became scared, deeply sad, and couldn't bring herself to go back to the hospital. In addition to not understanding what was going on with her, she also struggled significantly with guilt for not going back to the hospital. She felt like she was letting down her sister and her family, and she "knew" everyone else was thinking she was a terrible person. She was completely overwhelmed and definitely blindfolded on her emotional roller coaster, with no one at the controls to help it stop.

Based on the lesson I learned from her experience, I promised myself that I will do everything I possibly can to help people feel at peace with whatever their choice is about communicating with and/or visiting my care receivers. I don't know their past and what might be making them uncomfortable. I don't want to compound anyone's discomfort by making them feel bad if they don't have the capacity to participate in our experience. I do everything I can to support what they have capacity for, and I help them feel good about themselves with their choices. I also want to help as many people as possible make informed decisions, so they feel confident about their choices.

Even though Jack may no longer recognize the person greeting him, I see how his face lights up when they do. When someone talks with Jack on the phone, he gets a big smile on his face. When he gets shiny cards, he loves looking at them. We have a wonderful friend who regularly sends Jack unique, sparkly cards. I take them back to him every week and he enjoys them every time. His head may only remember in the moment, and his smile tells me his heart remembers.

I've learned to treasure the beauty of moments like these and create as many of them as I can. Whether someone has a broken leg or has a neurocognitive disorder, I focus on making each moment as positive as possible.

The Grace of Space

As I continued to remove responsibilities from Jack's list and add them to mine, I spent increasing amounts of his waking time caring for him only. Other tasks shifted to after he went to bed or before he awoke. I've always been able to manage without much sleep, so I didn't think this would be an issue.

One day, I found myself getting irritated by what Jack was doing. I knew he wasn't intentionally doing things to irritate me, and I was still irritated. I remember very clearly having lunch with Jack and he dropped potato chips on the floor several times. I snapped at him and asked him why he wasn't paying attention. When I did that, I shocked myself. That's not like me, and Jack definitely didn't deserve my response; he wouldn't do that if he could help it. I realized that I wasn't practicing what I call the "grace of space".

I define the "grace of space" as the moment between when something happens and my conscious choice about how I feel, think and act. I've learned, for me, if I'm too tired, I don't practice giving myself that space. I react and respond unconsciously, potentially without care and compassion. When I see that I'm losing my grace of space, it's a reminder to practice some self-care. Am I getting enough sleep? Am I getting the support I need to stay balanced so I'm not overwhelmed mentally, emotionally, or physically? Is there something going on I don't know how to deal with? When I have the grace of space, I am able to stay present and act from choice.

It's Better to Give When They Can Receive

I study a personality informing assessment called the Enneagram[35] that's still relevant today even though it was created more than one thousand years ago. It explains that there are nine main personality types, and each of us is primarily one of them. Our personality type informs how we naturally see the world, how we think, how we feel, how we interact with others, how we deal with stress and how we make decisions. No type is right or wrong, better or worse; they're just different. As a care giver, one of the greatest gifts of the Enneagram is that it helps me understand why my perspective, the perspective of my care receiver, and the perspectives of others, can be so different.

Whether or not you focus on any kind of personality trait education, honoring the fact that we are all wired with different points of view expands the potential of your curiosity, compassion, perspective, understanding, respect, and acceptance. Since learning the Enneagram, I know how I'm most likely to react under stress. It teaches me about options for consciously choosing my behavior rather than allowing my fears and emotions to unconsciously drive them. I now embrace the differences of perspective between myself, my care receiver or another member of our care support team. We are then able to embrace our multiple perspectives. In my experiences, the enneagram information remains accurate even as my care receiver's health changes. It's been most helpful for me when I know I need to do something that will be challenging for them.

Before I became aware of how powerful our natural way of viewing our worlds is for how we receive and provide information and care, I knew we all had our own personalities. Some of us get along easily and others not so well. I knew that some people, for example, liked to really think things through before taking action, some people always seemed to focus on the worst possible scenarios, and some people reacted strongly under stress. Others seemed to have the ability of staying calm. I hadn't connected all of that with how valuable my help would be with this knowledge— especially under stress and fear.

There was a woman in one of our care support meetings who would share her troubles and seemed resistant to accept anyone's advice. When she asked me about what I'd gone through, I immediately wanted to provide help, eagerly sharing something we'd learned and encouraging her to try it. She would start every response with a "Yeah, but..." Each time I, or anyone else, offered a suggestion, she would have a reason why it wouldn't work. Many of us in our care support meeting would become frustrated, yet we also wanted to help. On the flipside, she would share lessons she had learned and offer them to others in order to help.

Once I learned the basics of the Enneagram, I realized her personality style resisted receiving information because she interpreted it as being told what to do, even if it's in the spirit of helpfulness.

My husband, Jack, taught me a valuable lesson about offering advice. "The best time to offer advice is right after someone actually asks for it." I have now added the caveats:

"...and actually wants it."

"...and I'm the right person to offer it."

"...and I am able to offer it in a way it can be effectively received."

I was offering advice from the perspective of how valuable a lesson had been for me, not considering how she would receive it, or if she actually wanted it. These two lessons have helped me have more positive experiences and fewer frustrations every day. When I observe that someone would benefit from lessons I've learned, I find out first if they actually want guidance. If they don't, that's okay with me. Just because I'm passionate about helping everyone doesn't mean they have to want my support, that I have what they need, or that I'm the best person to provide it. If they do want support, I work with them to learn how to best help them receive, and benefit from, what I'm sharing.

Changing my approach with the woman in our support group made a huge difference for me, for others in our group, and for her. There were times when I could now hear in her voice that she wasn't asking for guidance, she was just sharing her circumstances. In those times we just listened. When she did ask for guidance, I didn't respond with a suggestion of what she could try. I simply explained what we did, why we did it, and how it worked for us. There was no reason for her to explain why it wouldn't work for her, I wasn't asking her to try it. Several others in our group adopted the same approach and another member of our group added an additional approach, she would simply ask this woman if she wanted our guidance or just wanted to be heard. These considerations have continued to be very helpful for us.

As a result, we weren't frustrated anymore. The woman quit providing reasons why our advice wouldn't work for her. On several occasions, she shared that she'd tried one of our ideas and it had worked.

With this as my lens through which I discern my advice-giving, I'm able to peacefully balance my natural passion to help everyone with whether or not someone wants advice - and if I'm the right person to provide it.

The Power of Music

I've previously referenced the power of music in the care experience, where we have seen signs of its impact in even the tiniest of reactions and the strength of its impact in the moment. In my early roles of caregiving, I didn't know how incredibly valuable and magical music is for therapy and support. I've witnessed it many times now and for the benefit of my care receiver and I, we won't live without it. The power of music therapy to help those with neurocognitive disorders, traumatic injuries, disabilities, congenital disorders, and stress is well documented. There are also a variety of resources available. For example, I have learned that since key brain areas linked to musical memory are relatively undamaged by Alzheimer's, music is great activity every day.[36]

I first became aware of the power of music when our family was raising horses. We kept our horses at a barn where there was a young woman (I'll use the name Sally) who had received a traumatic brain injury from a serious accident. Her life passion was horses and while her accident had changed the type of experience she would have, it didn't prevent horses from being one of the most successful components of her rehabilitation.

One result of her accident was a periodic uncontrollable movement disorder that would cause her horse to become startled and move suddenly. This prevented Sally from being allowed around her beloved horse or from benefitting from equine therapy[37]. Sally's family was committed to her having as normal a life as possible and being able to be participating in something she was so passionate about. Sally's horse trainer and her physical therapist worked together to determine songs that would soothe both Sally and her horse (yes, it's also successful therapy for horses). When it came time for her session, those of us at the barn would stand quietly around, mesmerized by what they were doing together for Sally and her horse.

The selected music would begin to play over the speakers in the barn. After a few minutes of listening to the music, Sally's movements seemed to lessen and she would roll her wheelchair up to her horse, a little in front of her horse's shoulder so her horse could see her most clearly. Sally would just sit for a few minutes, breathing deeply. She would then put her arm out to touch the palm of her hand to her horse. During this time, those of us watching would look at each other in amazement; Sally had no spasmodic movements and her horse remained still. Several visits later, the therapist had Sally rub her horse's face. Again, there were no spasmodic movements and her horse stood calmly. There were more successes after that.

It didn't occur to me to ask if they used the music with Sally's other rehabilitation, so I don't know anything else. I do know the use of music worked very well for Sally and her horse. I wish I had connected the power of music to comfort Mary, but I didn't. I try not to miss lessons like this anymore!

My mother-in-love, Donna, very successfully used music therapy to help my dad stay calm. She had soft music playing in their home from the time they woke up in the morning until they went to bed at night. When I shared Jack's diagnosis with her, one of the first things Donna encouraged me to do was begin playing music in our home. It was great guidance and while it didn't work for every situation, it did help Jack much of the time. My experiences with Jack and music, especially now that he is living in memory care, are truly powerful and seemingly magical. There are also many amazing and touching experiences with other residents.

I've mentioned the musicians who frequently come into Jack's memory care unit to play familiar songs for the residents. While singing, the musicians walk to each resident, acknowledging each one individually. The residents sing along, dance, and engage with the music. They feel special and included; everyone looks forward to it. On Sunday mornings, there is a religious service in our memory care unit. Several hymns are sung at the beginning and end of the service. It's wonderful to see how many residents still know the words to the hymns.

Many of Jack's memories aren't accessible to him anymore; this is absolutely not the case with music! When a hymn begins to play, Jack begins singing the correct words right away. One of the funniest moments was when a hymn began playing that is often played during the time when financial offerings are collected in the catholic church. Jack immediately reached into his pocket for his wallet to get out his money for the collection. Not finding his wallet, he turned to me and said in a startled tone: "I don't have my money for the collection." Using compassionate truth, I explained we had mailed them a check. He immediately calmed, and resumed singing the hymn from memory, while I enjoyed the multiple connections the music made for him.

Having now studied the power and impact of music, as well as Dr. Pearsall's work with the brain of the heart, I use the time when music is playing to tell Jack how much I love him. (No, not during the church service, all the other times though!) I kneel in front of him, look directly into his eyes, get a big smile on my face, tell him how much I love him and how much he means to me.

When music isn't playing, it's sometimes difficult for him to either focus on my face or look me in the eyes. With music, his face lights up every time, he looks me directly in the eyes, and he tells me how much he loves me. There will be a day when he doesn't have capacity to do this anymore and I completely accept it; I know his heart.

Help is All Around Me and I Need All of it I Can Get!

My first two roles of care support happened before the Internet, so people didn't have a way to share personal issues publicly. I know what it's like to not know what I don't know, not know who or what to ask, and not know what to do. This is an example of riding the emotional roller coaster blindfolded every day! I've made it a focus of mine to recognize what will help my care receiver and/or me and stay attentive to opportunities for helping others.

I have an incredible amount of respect for how each person handles the sharing of their own diagnosis or that of their loved ones, how they engage with others, and how they choose to receive help. What breaks my heart is the stories people share who have struggled and suffered alone for so long because they were embarrassed to reach out, didn't want to inconvenience anyone, weren't sure how to get help, had a loved one who didn't want them to tell anyone, or who felt it was their responsibility to handle everything. I don't want any of these examples to be me or anyone else.

Advice from Experience
On many occasions, I've received what must have seemed like very simple help yet it has had a profound impact on my peace of mind as well as on the quality of care I'm providing. I once had the experience of Jack leaving the house when I wasn't aware of it. I was not prepared for this type of event. When it happened, I reached out to our support community. One of them suggested a double key deadbolt on the door and directed me to where they had purchased theirs. I had no idea those existed. It took less than one hour for me to buy one and install it. The member of our support community who had

provided the advice had already experienced what I had gone through, done the research for the best solution, and was glad to share it with me.

At the store from which I was purchasing the lock, I explained to the sales representative why I was purchasing it. He told me they had installed a double key deadbolt for his mom and when they did, they also bought a programmable lockbox for her house key to put by the front door. They gave the code to the police department so that in the case of an emergency, the police wouldn't have to break down the door. I now share about both the deadbolt and the lockbox when someone is in a similar situation. Help is all around us every day and people want to help.

Internet Help

Another time, I helped a friend learn how to use the search function on the Internet. She wanted to learn more about the specific diagnosis of her husband and she didn't know how to look it up. Something very simple for me was very helpful for her.

While we still struggle with scientific breakthroughs and cures for a variety of conditions that include neurocognitive disorders, traumatic injuries, disabilities, and congenital disorders, we have come a long way with cultural acceptance and inclusion. We embrace those who, like all of us, are perfectly imperfect. I talk openly about what we're going through so I can receive the understanding support of others. Technology provides me information in a variety of ways and brings connections from around the world. Whatever I'm searching for and whatever my preferred method of research and connection, there is help available to me every day, twenty-four hours a day.

This makes "Sense(s)"!

Help is all around me, coming from me, when I pay attention! When I began studying how we store memories, I learned that the more ways we connect with an experience the more connections are created in us. The better we remember it, even if we don't understand it at the time, the more we can recall it if the occasion arises. When I completely step into an experience with as many of my senses as possible, I help myself. I have found I do improve my memory of the experience!

In his 2003 book, *What Happy People Know*, author Dan Baker[38] explains:

> We don't describe the world we see—we see the world we describe...the stories we tell ourselves about our own lives eventually become our lives.

When I authentically connect with my experiences through as many of my senses as possible—sight, sound, smell, touch, and taste—I'm giving myself more opportunities to fully experience and remember the moment.

Websites are Great for Research, But Less as Replacements

I never grew out of the unquenchable curiosity of a child. I love learning and question things I'm curious about until I understand them. One of my friends calls me "Soogle" because I'm continuously looking things up. I look up definitions, synonyms and antonyms of words to make sure I clearly understand what they mean and how to use them. I research the diagnoses of my care receivers, the medications they are taking, symptoms and behaviors they are exhibiting, and how to become a more effective care giver.

I've learned to use Internet search engines and websites very intentionally and specifically for research—not for diagnosis, but for learning. It's helpful for discovering places to develop relationships, not to replace relationships. I've learned to use the Internet as one vital tool in my tool belt for being the best version of myself. I've learned for myself that, in areas where I don't have experience, becoming familiar with something is very helpful, especially in preparation for talking with an expert.

I've experienced taking my research and findings to doctors, who arrive at a completely different diagnosis based on knowledge I didn't have. The doctors appreciated my having done research because it improved the quality of our conversation and they appreciated my not using the Internet to tell them what I thought they should do.

I've conducted searches with results that vary so widely I can't make a reliable conclusion. I've also conducted searches and unearthed incredibly valuable information. Part of the value in information is knowing *how* to apply it to my situation, the reason I'm researching in the first place.

I've learned to conduct research about conducting research. I begin by asking those who've been on the journey before me for resources that work well for them. I ask members of support communities. I ask experts in their field. I ask doctors and nurses. I search websites directly associated with what I want to know.

A research "trap" I have fallen into on occasion is allowing my searches to take me out of the present, causing me to project into the future based on what "typical" results provide.

When I first learned of my grandmother's Alzheimer's diagnosis, I began doing research about the disease. I researched many areas of the disease including stages, symptoms, foods to eat, foods not to eat, what to say when talking with her, what not to do when I was with her.

There were both consistencies and inconsistencies. In some areas, my research gave me a clearer picture and in others, I became more confused than confident about what to do. For example, in studying the different stages of Alzheimer's, I found some expert sources talk about seven stages[39], while others mention three stages[40]. I realized I was trying to figure out where my grandmother's symptoms fit in the different stages. I got caught up trying to assess in which stage(s) she was rather than being present to her when I was with her.

The wise choice was to research the progression of the disease to begin to understand it and, when I was with my grandmother, her make my primary focus being present to her so I could make our time together the best for both of us. The stage she was in was not nearly as important as the moment she was in.

With technology as the foundation of my entire professional career, I appreciate how it simplifies access to information. It can also be a great connector. One result of my online research was discovering Facebook support groups[41] that provide a platform for asking questions, sharing frustrations and celebrations, receiving support, and talking live with other group members. During one of these live events, one of the women in the group explained she lived in Alaska and this group was her only live connection with others like her. I completely support this kind of facilitation, and I am glad technology today gives everyone access to a valuable, global opportunity for connection. There are also high-quality video meeting resources that provide great opportunities to connect.

This being said, I still find connecting in-person, when possible, valuable for a number of reasons. A few of these include being able to observe the body language of people who are and aren't participating. We make sure their needs are truly being met, are able to give a hug of support and encouragement and learn more about them before and after the meeting if they want to. One example of this was noticing a gentleman who had been a regular at our meeting who had missed several meetings. We reached out to him and learned he had become depressed and wasn't getting out anymore. We encouraged him to come back, told him how much he was missed and how much we cared. We offered to pick him up and bring him to our meetings. Just our reaching out to him and having him know how much we cared helped him feel better and he began returning to the meetings. We observed his body language more closely to get a sense of how he was feeling. We were able to support him through his depression, encouraged him to get professional help if he wanted it and made sure we would care for his wife as he received help so he would feel okay leaving her.

For a period of time, while I chose to accept more and more of the responsibilities in Jack's and our household's care, I invested less and less time reaching out to others in person and outside our home. I was in the Facebook group, I was researching online, and I wasn't next to others walking the journey with me.

When Jack and I both began going to support meetings, we were present with others, and connected in a more impactful way than I felt online. Some of our meetings involved care givers and care receivers meeting in different rooms. Some of our meetings were couples' meetings. The dynamic of us all leaning in to share our experiences and perspectives—like navigating the touchy situation of having the care receiver quit driving a car—is amazing and an incredible support. The group environment helps individuals feel safe being vulnerable, open, honest with their struggles and asking for help. In-person groups are also a wonderful opportunity for people to give back in gratitude for the help they have received.

I know sitting together in-person is not possible for everyone. If you don't have access to connecting face-to-face, I'm glad you have the opportunity to participate with others online and receive valuable support. If you do have the opportunity to sit with others, I encourage you to consider it. It's the meeting itself, the time before, the time after. It's someone who understands, handing you a tissue when your tears come. It's you being able to see someone at the table who doesn't know what to say and encouraging them to share. It's so much more than even this.

Elephants: The Parable, The Training, The Bite and "In The Room"

Elephants have played an important role in some of my most valuable life lessons, both in my roles of care support and in the rest of my life. From the parable of the elephant and the blind men, I have gained insights about the impact of each of us having unique perspectives. Learning how elephants used to be trained awakened me to valuable insights about reevaluating my beliefs to make sure they serve me today. I have found the phrase "the elephant in the room" is a perfect metaphor for one of the most challenging and important components of relationships and of significant changes in our lives.

Elephants, known for their incredible memories, are also frequently recognized as one of the symbols associated with Alzheimer's disease[42]. When I see them, I have the opportunity to be reminded of valuable lessons in navigating my caregiving journey of love every day.

The Parable of the Elephant and the Blind Men
There is an Indian parable about six blind men who come across an elephant[43]. Each man experiences only one part of the elephant and that becomes his reality of the elephant. None of the six has a clear picture of the elephant as a whole. When they each share their perspective, they all disagree, and they argue about who is right and who is wrong about what the elephant is like.

Lessons I use from this parable include:

- As an encouragement for me to learn as much as I can and become confident in my perspective.
- Remain ever curious and open-minded to considering, without judgement, other perspectives. I focus on remembering that different perspectives are not right or wrong, they are different.
- I have the choice to maintain my perspective or modify it.
- Develop new collective perspectives if they are more valuable than the individual perspectives of each of us.

This is another important reason why I don't use the labels others use without understanding their definition and gaining clarity for myself. Each of the six men experienced an elephant. If I just accept one person's perspective without developing my own perspective with clarity, I may be missing the rest of the elephant—and the best experience possible.

Elephant Training

In recent years, elephant training has changed to an approach using positive feedback[44]. Previously, a less humane method was used. I feel the history of elephant training applies directly to my perspective around care support. I realized I had been trained, and trained myself, like the old style of elephant training and, just as it's not right for elephants anymore, it's not right for me anymore either.

Historically, young elephants were tethered to a stake in the ground by a long rope attached to their leg[45]. While they are very young, the rope is strong enough to keep them from escaping. They struggle and can't detach themselves. After a while, they accept their reality and believe they can't escape. Once they have accepted their reality, they don't reexamine it. As they grow, they become much stronger than the rope and because they believe the rope is stronger than they are, they don't test it to reevaluate if it's still accurate.

Throughout my life, I have developed my beliefs from lessons I've learned. The story of how baby elephants were trained sparked an incredible awakening in me. I realized I had not been reevaluating lessons I'd learned at other times in my life to identify if they still served me. I was still tethered to the beliefs of early lessons. I want to make conscious choices about keeping or discarding old beliefs in light of if/how they serve me best now. I had to be willing to discard old beliefs, even if those lessons were taught to me from a place of love and safety.

Here are two examples of this:

"Look both ways before you cross the street." As a young child, everyone told me this! I was told this time and time again for what seemed like years! I was trained to pay attention to my surroundings and make sure I was safe before stepping into the street or parking lot. This was taught to me from a place of love to keep me safe. This training became my unconscious behavior pattern and has saved my life multiple times, even in just the past several years! With so many people distracted by mobile devices, some are not paying close attention. It's a good thing this is my automatic pattern. I choose to keep this old lesson.

"Don't talk to strangers." I was taught this whenever we went shopping, to events, parks, movies, anywhere there would be strangers. Like the first example, this lesson was taught out of love and safety and became an unconscious behavior pattern. As an adult, my role in sales requires me to talk with strangers every day. When I became aware of my unconscious programming, I had sudden clarity and realized the absolute of "not talking to strangers" no longer served me. I wanted to engage with people who I had not yet met! While I honor the training of my childhood, I now make conscious choices with my new perspective that serves me very well today.

How does this process of reevaluation help me in my roles of care support every day? I stay present. I focus on how I am supporting my care receiver to make sure they are the most comfortable they can be at the moment and that I am staying in balance.

For example, I observe how my care receiver is experiencing each component of their day. I look at them with "fresh eyes" observing changes. I don't necessarily consider "absolutes" in caregiving, I consider context. I adapt my care when there are changes and take my lead from their needs and abilities.

I observe and ask questions of other care support providers in order to make sure they are getting the support they need and are able to do their job the best way possible. It's important for me to ensure they can adapt and respond appropriately to changes in my care receiver. Because there are periodic changes in my care receiver, I check in with them on a frequent basis.

Here is one example that encompasses three roles: Walking. Jack has always enjoyed walking. He used to walk 4–5 miles on a daily basis. This has diminished in the past year. I observed other residents in the memory care community where he lives and noticed some of them experiencing difficulty with their balance, getting out of chairs, and walking. I have learned this also leads to a lack of continence.

1. **My Support:** Focusing on my goals for Jack to be safe and in an environment that supports his happiness, I focus intentionally on keeping him as healthy as possible. I observe him closely to monitor his balance, ease of walking, and getting up out of chairs. In the beginning of our time in the memory care community, I tried to get Jack to lift light weights—please laugh with me. It wasn't successful at all. Instead, we focus on walking quite a bit. (A tip here. With diminishing short-term memory, we walk awhile and take a break. We perhaps sit a few minutes or get something to drink. I then ask Jack if he'd like to go for a walk and he says "yes." We get more exercise because we break it into

shorter segments, and he gets to repeat something he enjoys as if we're doing it for the first time that day.)

2. **My care receiver:** One day, I noticed Jack beginning to shuffle his feet rather than picking them up. I saw a correlation between his lack of interest in exercise when I asked him, and the beginning of shuffling. Having learned previously that I'm not the best instructor for him, I reached out to community family members to find the name of a trainer who worked well with their care receivers.

3. **Other care support providers:** Through our community, I was introduced to an amazing trainer who Jack is glad to exercise with. The trainer and I worked together with Jack so the trainer would learn how to best communicate with Jack and what would trigger him. We talked about my goals for Jack so the trainer had direction. Yep, they work great together! Jack will do anything for his trainer and the proof is in the results. Jack is able to get up out of chairs easily, his balance is good, and he picks up his feet when he walks.

The Bite

I have often heard, and used, variations of the ancient proverb about being deliberate with things that are difficult by taking them one step at a time: "When eating an elephant take one bite at a time[46]." I use the elephant as a reminder every day of how I focus on components of my responsibilities of care support. The entirety of care support responsibilities can be overwhelming. If I begin to feel this way, I observe and study it.

I work to break it down into smaller and more manageable "bites" until they aren't overwhelming. When I am able to view a situation objectively, and not react from ego and/or emotion, I am able to make conscious choices, act, and move on.

I don't have to be the only one "eating" the elephant. When breaking down my care support responsibilities, I evaluate who the most qualified person is to provide each component of support.

"In The Room"

The phrase "the elephant in the room[47]" is a figure of speech that represents a major issue or concern that is obvious to everyone and not discussed because it is uncomfortable or unpleasant. Through my many years of experience in roles of care support, I have learned there are a lot of elephants in the rooms! Most of the time, a group of elephants is called a herd, a parade, or a memory[48]. In this case, any one of the "elephants", and certainly the whole group of "elephants," is called overwhelm!

Addressing these helps me, my care receiver, and anyone else involved, make informed decisions, create the space for peace of mind, and reduce anxiety.

"Elephants" may be many different things including people and things. The people may be us, it may be members of our family, it may be friends, it may be work or community associates, and it may be professionals we rely on. The things may include the disease itself, impacts of the disease, and conversations we aren't used to having. For example, conversations are sometimes about topics in which we don't have experience. They are sometimes about topics we'd rather avoid. They sometimes involve complex family dynamics.

Figuring out how to address the "elephants" can be awkward, messy, and uncomfortable.

I'm very fortunate to have learned valuable lessons from others in our support group meetings about addressing the "elephants." Many of the stories shared were raw and powerful. They helped me see that, no matter how awkward and uncomfortable it is to deal with the "elephants," it's much better than the results of not addressing them or delaying addressing them. I've heard example after example where avoiding these "elephants" led to serious and negative relationship, safety, financial, medical, and legal impacts. These lessons inspired me to take action so that our impacts are positive.

The list of "elephants" will be different for everyone. Some of the "elephants" I've addressed include:

- Talking about the disease diagnosis, traumatic event, or specific condition.
- Fears about what will happen. This is on the mind of the person who has received their diagnosis, everyone in their family, and those in their circle of support.
- Recognizing symptoms of a disease in a friend or loved one before anyone else may even be aware of it or before it's been discussed.
- Happiness guilt.
- Taking away "freedoms," including driving.
- Changes in physical relationships.
- Taking on responsibilities in areas in which I don't have experience and/or interest.
- Making changes in our environment that support my care receiver being safe.
- Needing additional support.

- What to do in case of emergencies including acts of nature and caregiver health crises.
- Finances, including having enough resources, managing them, and paying bills.
- Insurance.
- Children providing personal care for parents.
- Legal matters including power of attorney, wills, ownership of assets, advance directives to refuse care (ADRT).
- Family disagreements about care responsibilities and options.
- Care support emotions.
- Care giver self-care and/or lack thereof.
- Funerals.
- Organ donation for research or transplant.
- The grieving process.

Bringing the "Elephants" Together

I bring together the elephant parable, training, proverb, and expression to help me navigate my care support journey with my care receiver.

First, focusing on the parable of the six blind men and the elephant, I've learned we bring our own perspective to each item on our list. I've learned there are a variety of human dynamics[49] considerations that impact how we navigate each item. It's important for me to be aware of these because the items may not have the same importance or emotional charge for each of us. I don't want to assume anything. I make sure I honor my care receiver's considerations and give him/her the opportunity to honor mine. Some of the things I consider, in order for us to have our most valuable conversations, include our:

- Natural personality styles.
- Perspectives.
- Previous experiences and the emotions surrounding them.
- Status of current relationships.
- Family dynamics.
- Health considerations—physical, emotional, and psychological.
- Beliefs.
- Religious precepts, doctrines, laws and rules.

Second, reflecting on the training of elephants, I evaluate my beliefs in each area. I want to make sure they serve me where I am today. I consider how I will talk with my care receiver to help them evaluate their beliefs. This is another area where I have had conversations with others before having my conversation with my care receiver so I can walk through the conversation with someone else first. One of the most significant disagreements I've heard about from other support group members and their care receivers is in the area of additional care, either in-home or moving to a support facility. Walking through this with someone else first helps me consider my beliefs and theirs as I frame our conversation.

Third, using the proverb about eating the elephant one bite at a time, I decide how I want to separate the "elephants in the room" into separate rooms. This is also known as breaking down my list of concerns into smaller and smaller, manageable components, until I lose my sense of overwhelm and imbalance. One example of this was the issue of having Jack quit driving. I researched everything I could about legal considerations of individuals driving if they have a diagnosis of a type of Dementia. I contacted our Doctor's office and spoke with a member of their staff about how they recommend this issue be addressed, and I spoke with our support group.

I learned the Doctor was supposed to take Jack's driver's license from him and report him to the state. I learned that if someone drives after having received the diagnosis and they are in an accident, even if they are not at fault, and it becomes known they have the diagnosis, we could be sued; I was provided several examples of this. I broke this situation down into multiple pieces:

- How will Jack feel about losing his independence?
- How should this be addressed?
- Who should address it?
- When is the best time to address it?
- What adjustments do I need to make to ensure Jack doesn't feel uncomfortable asking to be driven somewhere or feel a loss of freedom when he can't just pick up the keys and go?
- What can I do ahead of time to reduce his anxiety before he actually has it?

I look at the list in its entirety, knowing that any one of the items on the list could be overwhelming by itself. I separate the items in groups that are logical to me. I sometimes put the same item in multiple groups to help me create the clarity necessary for optimal success. Here are examples of several of the groupings I create:

- Urgent: Items we need to address while both my care receiver and I have capacity to discuss them. This has included legal items in which we both have to participate and sign. In the case of our wills, for example, it includes items that involve our children.

- Complex: Items we need to process on multiple levels and that include learning about them and/or having a variety of conversations over a period of time. These can be items:
- We have had little or no experience with.
- We haven't previously talked about. In the case of second marriages, we may not know our spouse's previous experience with certain issues.
- Requiring professional assistance to complete: financial, medical, or legal.
- We will share with our family once we make our decisions. Among these are our advance directives, wills, powers of attorney, organ donation and funeral wishes.
- Emotional: Learning from others who have dealt with certain issues will give us insight on how to have potentially emotional conversations. This group may include fears about what will happen, taking away "freedoms" like driving, and needing additional support. These are also items where it may be helpful for one of us to have a conversation with someone else before we have the conversation together.
- Awkward: Lastly, some of the "elephants in the room" are just awkward. While there isn't an easy way to address them, it is necessary to do so. These include items like:
- Changes in physical and intimate relationships.
- Family members providing personal care for other family members.

Using the example of discontinuing his driving, it included some of each of these.

It was urgent because legally he wasn't supposed to be driving anymore.

It was complex with many different factors to be considered before determining what I would do and who would be involved.

It was emotional because Jack had been driving more than fifty years and this was a very tangible recognition of the magnitude of this disease, even while he had very few symptoms. He could consider this a significant loss of freedom.

It was awkward. I had not dealt with this before personally. My grandmother had been resistant to discontinuing driving. She only drove a few places and they were all close to where she lived. My uncle had put a sign in the back window of her car with his contact information on it. One day, as she drove to church, she lost her way. She pulled to the side of the street, someone contacted my uncle, and she gave him her keys. My Dad, and two other friends I was providing support for, willingly gave up their keys. In support meetings I had heard really rough stories of the struggles in this area.

I created a plan, contacted his doctor, asked him to have the conversation with Jack and leverage the issue of being sued if there was an accident. Our doctor brought up the topic, spoke with Jack in the most compassionate way, and explained the considerations to him. Jack handed me the keys and it was never an issue. I did make sure he always had a ride, I was positive and enthusiastic about driving him, and would sometimes make up errands so we could go out in the car.

Jack and I were fortunate to have visited multiple friends who had made changes in their living arrangements to support their additional needs. We were able to see how these changes helped them thrive in their day-to-day lives. We had also seen the significant and deeply emotional struggles of one couple who was in complete disagreement in this area. In another "elephant" conversation, Jack and I talked about our beliefs based on the positive experiences we'd observed and the couple who was struggling so much. We agreed we would be supportive of each other in this area. This made our hard conversations easier and, when it became obvious it was time for Jack to move into a facility that provided the professional care he needed, I knew it was something he had already agreed would be the right decision.

Step 5: Finding Hope

Massive acceptance and radical presence give me the gift of living each moment from its greatest potential.

Hope is not a dream, hope is potential.

I used to say I "hoped" for something. As with many other words, I hadn't looked up its definition to understand it accurately for myself and gain clarity on what it means in my life. The dictionary definition for hope is "To cherish a desire with anticipation, to want something to happen or be true, to expect with confidence, to trust[50]."

I have now learned what hope means for me. Hope helps motivate and sustain me. Hope helps me maintain a positive attitude. Hope gives me strength.

I have found hope. It is why I know I will never again feel helpless and lost. I know that even when I stumble in my emotions, thoughts, feelings, and actions, the lessons I am learning are a gift that come wrapped in resilience and the perseverance to keep going. Hope helps me find meaning and purpose in the experiences of my life.

In his book, *Man's Search for Meaning*, psychologist and Holocaust survivor, Viktor Frankl, explains the importance of finding meaning and purpose in our experiences. This is so we find our will to live beyond mere survival and learn to be happy, satisfied, and fulfilled.

What man actually needs is not a tensionless state but rather the striving and struggling for some goal worthy of him. What he needs is not the discharge of tension at any cost, but the call of a potential meaning waiting to be fulfilled by him[51].

An excerpt of the lyrics of the song *You'll Never Walk Alone*, from the 1945 Rogers & Hammerstein musical Carousel[52], reflects the concept of hope for me:

When you walk through a storm
Hold your head up high
And don't be afraid of the dark.
Walk on through the wind,
Walk on through the rain,
Tho' your dreams be tossed and blown.
Walk on, walk on
With hope in your heart
And you'll never walk alone,
You'll never walk alone.

The key to my hope is my practice of *massive acceptance* and *radical presence*.

Acceptance Without The Need to Understand

While I'm sure I was aware of, and practiced, acceptance earlier in my life, I was in junior high school science class the first time it became a focus for me. We were studying space and our teacher, Mr. Keyton, introduced infinity. Everyone else in the room wrote down notes about infinity and moved on. It completely threw me off balance.

Infinity? No beginning and no end? How can that be? Everything has to begin somewhere. How do we know there is no beginning? How do we know it doesn't end? I remember asking several questions and, while I don't remember the answers, I remember they did nothing to help me. I went home from school that day very distracted, confused, and frustrated. That night at dinner with my parents and older brother, I brought up learning about infinity that day. They were fine with the concept of infinity, and thought I was too, until I completely broke down in tears. I went through my questions with them, and I do remember them explaining there are some things we don't yet know everything about. They were trying to be supportive, but their answers didn't help me.

For several days, I struggled with having questions and no answers. One day, Mr. Keyton asked if I had time to stop by class for a few minutes after school. When I did, he asked me to sit down at my desk, take out a piece of paper and my pencil, and write something down. He had me write, "There are things I just have to accept, even if I don't understand them." I kept that paper with me for many years.

Amazingly, this flipped a switch for me. I now had a place to put what I couldn't understand. It wasn't just a series of questions with no answers bouncing around, causing me to become overwhelmed. It meant I had legitimate questions and I didn't have to understand them or the answers right then, or maybe ever. I had the gift of peace knowing it was ok to accept them without the need to understand them.

I've had many experiences that resulted in lessons I didn't understand at the time. I consciously accepted them, "tagged" them, and filed them away. These lessons have come back through the years when the right context arose. They helped me understand an experience.

There have been times over the years when I would struggle to accept a situation in its entirety. I could accept parts of it, breaking it down into smaller and smaller pieces until I found the areas I could accept. However, in studying "acceptance," I learned an additional requirement of acceptance—it doesn't work in parts. I'm either all in or I'm all out. I either accept completely or I don't accept at all.

For me, the greatest gift of acceptance in its entirety is that it's the same for every experience, regardless of its importance. As I was learning how to apply this kind of acceptance, I came up with a two-part, fill-in-the-blank exercise. It helps me practice acceptance because I see on paper, and, for me, say out loud, that which I am considering applying acceptance.

I start by looking at the specific events I don't know how to accept and providing the reason why I don't.

Statement One: "I don't accept _____, because _____."

When I look at my situation through the intentional focus of this statement, I realize I actually do choose to accept it! Based on this realization, I then ask myself another fill- in-the-blank statement that gives me a positive foundation for the meaning of and purpose for the situation.

Statement Two: "I do accept _____, and _____."

This led to modifying my belief about acceptance: I accept without the need to understand. This brings me peace and freedom. I accept things completely and don't fight them, even if I don't understand them. I gain the peace of mind that creates a freedom to choose my next steps and my attitude. I am not locked into fighting what already is because I want it to be different. I don't define hope as wishing for a different outcome or reality. I use hope to strengthen me in what is actually occurring.

Jack had been solving crossword puzzles almost daily for more than forty years. He's a person who could complete the New York Times Sunday crossword puzzle using an ink pen, without looking up the answers. It would amaze me to watch him. He would also complete the daily puzzles in our local paper in a matter of minutes.

A little over a year after he was diagnosed with a type of dementia, I noticed Jack wasn't completing the daily puzzles or the New York Times puzzles anymore. He would still attempt them and filled in fewer and fewer words. That was one of the first major signs to me of his disease's progression. I walked through my fill-in-the-blank acceptance exercise.

Statement One:

I don't accept that Jack can't complete the crossword puzzles anymore because he's been able to do them so easily for many years. Frontotemporal dementia is supposed to impact other brain functions.

Statement Two:

I do accept that Jack can't complete the crossword puzzles, and I will look for things he can do instead that bring him enjoyment. There are nuances and differences with each type of dementia and with each diagnosed person; these make each experience unique.

Massive Acceptance

My dad's diagnosis of a type of dementia was a significant event in our lives. I needed an additional categorization of acceptance to separate the acceptance of such significant events from smaller experiences in which I could more easily accept and move on. I needed a more all-encompassing type of acceptance.

I knew that I could quickly lose myself when a significant event occurred, even though I had put measures in place to prevent that from happening. I wanted to make sure I reminded myself of my acceptance and continuously both kept watch of it and practiced it. Therefore, it would be available to me when major events arose that would threaten to throw me off balance. I wanted to make sure that in those moments I could recognize if I was beginning to feel overwhelmed and then get myself in balance as quickly and healthily as possible.

While I accepted my dad's diagnosis without the need to understand why it was happening, I wanted more than just acceptance. It was important for me to find its meaning and purpose in my life so I could live from that place. I wanted the experience to create the most positive impact possible in my life and help me do my best to support my dad, Donna and others who were caring for my dad.

I wrote out words that represented how providing care for him would be an all-encompassing task. Several of the many I wrote included: *immense, enormous, gigantic.* I learned these are synonyms for the word "massive[53]."

In order for me to fully accept our journey, find its purpose, and maximize its positive impact in our lives, I learned it is important for me to continuously practice *massive acceptance*.

Radical Presence

In my life with Jack, my purpose is for him to live his life knowing he is truly loved. When he was diagnosed, I became intentional about two things I'd been doing throughout our relationship:

- Keep him safe.
- Help create and support the environment that provides his best opportunities for his happiness.

Being vigilant and practicing massive acceptance allows me to stay thoroughly, completely, and utterly focused on exactly what is going on in the moment. I have this focus in my feelings, thoughts, emotions, and actions. This is *radical presence*.

Tennis Lessons

I play tennis. I began with lessons. My instructor taught me how to hold the racket, position my feet, and move the racket through its proper motion. We practiced each component multiple times. He then began gently tossing tennis balls to me so I could put all the components together and practice hitting the balls. As quickly as I could, I went through, in my mind, each of the elements the instructor had explained.

Picture balls going everywhere but back at the instructor! Picture me repeating each of my instructions with each stroke. I was mechanically repeating what I had been taught. It wasn't natural to me. I did a few things right, and I'd forgotten some of the other components. I didn't have any reference point for what it should feel like when it all came together.

My instructor kept gently tossing the balls to me. After many attempts, all of a sudden, a ball connected with my racket. The ball went over the net and landed exactly where it was meant to go. I got it! I had stopped mechanically trying to remember each component. Through these repeated actions, my brain had made the connections for this activity and developed long-lasting muscle memory. It could be now be repeated automatically and almost without thought[54].

Through practicing and practicing, I learned what it felt like to allow the experience instead of trying to mechanically create it. I finally had context. I no longer needed to focus on each of the components. I became present to the ball. The more I practiced, being present became easier and easier. I could process more, add more skills, and I could achieve more. Did that mean I hit every ball correctly? Absolutely not. It did mean I could learn from what did not turn out the way I anticipated and move forward with trying to improve. It meant I could take conscious action to make adjustments and stay in the game. It also meant I wasn't overwhelmed.

Practicing radical presence is like this for me. The more I practice it, the less mechanical it becomes. The more I learn about it, the more it becomes my unconscious pattern of behavior. I am able to observe, process more, and develop more skills. I feel balanced and confident so that when, like with tennis, the outcome is not what I anticipate, I make adjustments and stay present. I'm not overwhelmed.

Massive acceptance awakens me to the potential of my experience. Radical presence gives me clarity in the fullness of my experience.

The Practice of Massive Acceptance and Radical Presence

Practicing massive acceptance and radical presence both positions and prepares me for also stepping into the perspective of my care receiver. It supports me in meeting them where they are, in whatever type of moment they are experiencing. It opens my mind to trying to understand how they are thinking and feeling, through the lens of empathy. It strengthens me to take the right actions and help them from a place of deep compassion.

When I'm practicing massive acceptance and radical presence, I'm able to stay objective. I'm not projecting through fear or uncertainty what "might be." I'm not making judgements. I'm not looking at beautiful past memories, sad that they won't be recreated. Instead, I see their beauty, have gratitude for them and appreciate being reminded of them. I'm also living each experience through the lens of how I see it, not how someone else defines it.

Practicing massive acceptance and radical presence keeps me from reacting unintentionally to the experiences of my care receiver. Even during the most challenging moments, I'm able to stay focused, try to step into their perspective, and take positive action through conscious choices. This is where continuous lessons from support communities and studying experts—including Teepa Snow[55]—equip me with options I would not have known to consider.

One of the most powerful lessons I have learned from Teepa Snow is how to get my care receiver to shift their attention from one situation to another. While this is the traditional definition of redirection, what Teepa teaches is so much more.

Our care receiver is in some form of emotional distress. We meet them where they are. We honor them and we validate them. We then gently move their attention away from something that may be dangerous or risky for them or difficult for us. We do this one small step at a time, matching their body language, acknowledging them, and participating with them. Rather than ask them yes or no questions, we ask questions with simple choices; *"Is it this (whatever one choice is) or that (whatever is the other choice)?"*

Here is one example of small steps you (You) can use. This would occur when your care receiver (CR) is frustrated and says they want to go home.

You: You are right. I'm sure it is frustrating. I know you want to go home.

CR: Yes, I want to go home.

You: I bet you have a beautiful home. Is it a big home or a small home?

CR: It's a big home.

You: I bet you have wonderful meals in your kitchen. Do you have a coffee pot or a tea pot?

CR: A coffee pot.

You: A coffee pot! I love coffee! Would you like to come with me to get a cup of coffee or eat a cookie?

I've learned a lot from Teepa and her team through her company, Positive Approach® to Care[56]. What she teaches is working for my care receivers and me, which gives me peace of mind, especially when something happens and I don't know what to do. I appreciate Teepa's positive and compassionate strategies because the techniques she teaches are calming for both my care receiver and me. They also help me prevent stress and diminish my potential for compassion fatigue.

Practicing massive acceptance and radical presence gives me both permission—and the requirement—to focus on accepting how I am thinking and feeling in the moment. I don't become emotionally charged with fear, anger, or frustration by their behavior. I let go of what I want in the moment in order to best support the needs of my care receiver.

Review: Completing the Lesson

Reviewing an experience has been hugely valuable for me. I find time to go back to the experience and review it. I honor my feelings and thoughts. I decide what my best actions are to ensure I maintain healthy balance in my life and I look for lessons.

Learning from the Deadbolt

Earlier, I shared my lesson about the double key deadbolt. Here is more of that story. Before I learned about the double key deadbolt for our front door, Jack and I were having "quiet time." We would sit together, say prayers, and then have a period of meditation. One afternoon, you guessed it, I actually fell asleep. Of course, he did what he has never done before, he went downstairs and left the house. When I woke up, I was in a panic. I didn't know where he had gone. I had registered his information with the police department so I knew I could call them at any moment. I then stopped. I took a deep breath. I collected myself. I put myself in his shoes.

Jack was walking around and had no idea where he was. How was he feeling? He was probably unsure about where he was and where to go, and not frightened. He was in our neighborhood and he was used to taking long walks in our neighborhood. What was he thinking? *I'm on a walk around our neighborhood.* I saw that he could only have been gone for ten minutes, so he probably hadn't gone far, and may not even have become concerned. I got in our car and drove around the neighborhood looking for him. I found no sign of him. Naturally, one of our afternoon storms began right then and it started to rain. That would definitely cause him concern. I drove around the opposite direction in case I'd missed him. There he was, standing in front of one of our neighbors' garage doors.

I took a deep breath. I put a big smile on my face. I got out of the car. I looked him directly in the eyes and greeted him as if *I* had been the one gone. I asked if he'd enjoyed his regular walk around the neighborhood. I gave him a big hug and thanked him for loving me and waiting for me in the rain. I told him how much I loved him and appreciated him being there for me. I then asked him if he would get in the car so we could get out of the rain. He asked me why I didn't just put the garage door up and I (compassionate truth) told him I had to turn the car on to get the garage door opener to work. We were able to get home, I got him changed into dry clothes, and prepared him something to eat.

While he was eating, I went into our bathroom, sat on the floor, and began shaking. I let my emotions out; I had immediately been filled with fear for Jack. I then accepted that this was one of those events I knew could occur and hadn't thought to prepare for. I began looking for lessons from the experience.

I knew I could ask others what to do. I reminded myself that Jack was safe and happy. I said to myself out loud, "I now have a plan, it's okay to calm down." I was able to calm down. By accepting my feelings of fear for his safety, honoring them and dealing with them, I was able to prevent them from keeping me off-balance. The ability to get back in balance quickly gave me the opportunity for wise action from a rational place. I had a double key deadbolt on our front door within 24 hours. This definitely wasn't how I managed my emotions earlier on in my roles of care support. In my past, that fear would have stayed with me and continued to cloud my choices.

When I intentionally review the experience, I learn the rest of the lesson. This helps me put the experience in perspective. I am able to take away its initial emotional charge that may have clouded my clearly remembering valuable details to positively help me, and/or someone else, in the future.

Compassion Fatigue

"Everything can be taken from a man but one thing: the last of the human freedoms—to choose one's attitude in any given set of circumstances, to choose one's own way."
— *Viktor E. Frankl, Man's Search for Meaning*[57]

Others might not be able to take choice away from me, but I *can* give it away if I'm not careful.

In my earlier roles of care support, my focus kept shifting more and more to what I could do for my care receiver. What did they need? How did they feel? How else could I help them? I took on their pain and frustration as fuel to try harder and do more. I became exhausted emotionally, physically, mentally, and spiritually. This is riding the emotional roller coaster blindfolded, without coping mechanisms or tips and tricks to prevent overwhelm, and it led to compassion fatigue. I felt hopeless and helpless, accepting that my state was an unavoidable part of the journey.

When I became off-balance, I lost my belief that I had choice. I also lost my ability to do anything about it. In "Step 3: Tips & Tricks to Prevent Getting Overwhelmed," I introduced the importance of community as an external source of eyes and ears to help us recognize compassion fatigue. It's the disorder where we have focused so much for so long on helping others, we lose access to our physical, emotional and mental self-care. Compassion fatigue is considered a potential, natural result of working with people who have deeply distressing or disturbing experiences and is defined as a secondary traumatic stress disorder[58].

Symptoms of compassion fatigue may include apathy, poor self-care, mental and physical exhaustion, negative attitude, loss of belief in a vision, physical ailments, isolation, depression, and turning to substances to mask feelings[59]. If this is how I am living, I don't have the strength and confidence to access my purpose or make choices from a place of wellness and clarity.

Compassion fatigue is serious. I realized it's easy for me to develop because of my natural view of the world. I want everyone to be their best. I have concern for people who are suffering and I want to do whatever I can to help and support them. I want to understand them, so I know how best to provide my help and support. I am very willing to work hard and continue taking on additional responsibility so I can be more helpful. I'm happy in my life so I feel I can focus on helping others.

These very same positive traits are also the foundation of compassion fatigue. If I don't practice massive acceptance and radical presence in my life, I don't use the tools I've learned about maintaining a healthy balance. I may develop compassion fatigue without even realizing it.

Since beginning my practice of massive acceptance and radical presence, I no longer feel the symptoms of compassion fatigue. I feel connected with my purpose. I have balance in my life, even in moments of extreme challenge. I have access to resources that help me stay balanced during the ride of my emotional roller coaster and I live from conscious choice.

Fear and F.E.A.R.

My care receiver and I each have fears about what will happen based on what caused our journey to begin. Healthy fear is vital to our survival; it raises alarms for us to take action when something is not right[60]. It's when we aren't able to stay balanced that our fears become unhealthy and we aren't able to take wise action.

I learned an acronym for some fear: False Expectations Acting Real (F.E.A.R). When I hold fear inside me and I don't process it, much like a lottery draw machine, it bounces around inside my mind. The difference between the lottery draw machine and my F.E.A.R., is the draw machine only deals with what is real. When my F.E.A.R. bounces around in my mind and I don't know what to do, I begin to entertain worse and worse scenarios until I become completely out of balance, gripped by them, stopped from taking wise action because of them, and separated from what *is* real. This is what happened to my friend with her ill sister.

When I look at the journeys of my care receiver and myself as separate, I see each of us dealing with our fears differently, and rarely together. As a care giver, I didn't want to burden my care receiver with my fears, they had enough on their mind. Conversely, I've talked with many care receivers who say the exact same thing. They don't want to burden their loved ones with their fears, their loved ones have enough on their minds. They also say they don't know what to do with their fears. These fears are bigger than anything they've ever had before, and they don't know how to face them.

Monsters Under the Bed
When I was six years old, I began having nightmares about monsters under my bed. When I think back to that time, I clearly remember waking up in fear and screaming out loud. My mom or dad would come into my room, look under my bed, explain there were no monsters, and calm me until I went back to sleep. The nightmares continued. I can only imagine what this did to their sleep!

One night, my dad came into the room, turned on the lights and gently told me to get out of bed. I was petrified, and my dad was there to protect me. Holding my hand, he helped me look under the bed. I saw there were no monsters. We looked in the closet. There were no monsters. I went back to bed and the nightmares stopped. I was too young then to appreciate the lesson of facing my fears and realizing they weren't what I thought they were, and I have never forgotten this experience. I now have context for this lesson's importance in current experiences.

Are there bad experiences in my life? Definitely. Does everything turn out the way I want? Absolutely not. Do I understand why some things happen the way they do? No. What I don't do is let any of these become the F.E.A.R. that takes control of me, leaves me unbalanced or frozen in indecision.

Turning on The Light

Now, instead of keeping my fears from my care receiver and not wanting to draw attention to theirs, we face our fears together. We "turn on the light," and we talk about our concerns. I've learned to take the stopping emotion of fear and turn it into the productive emotion of curiosity. Through this curiosity, either I or my care receiver and I break down the situation into smaller and smaller pieces until we can figure out how to both face and take action on them without fear or F.E.A.R. We gain clarity on that which we do and do not have control over so we are free to focus on where we can do something. We create the space for peace and safety to replace our F.E.A.R.

My dad was an incredibly private person and talking about his feelings was difficult for him. The way I opened the door for him to talk about his fears was to tell him about one of mine and ask him for guidance. As he shared, I continued to ask him questions, and he was finally able to talk about his own fears. Once they were out in the open, we faced them together and we both felt peace; we both felt safe.

After my husband's diagnosis, I asked him of what he feared the most. He began crying and saying he didn't want to be a burden on me. I also began crying and told him I didn't want to be a burden on him. I told him I didn't know how to care for him, and I didn't want to do anything that might hurt him. We looked at each other and, at the same time, we began saying a prayer we had learned together:

"God, grant me the serenity to accept the things I cannot change, the courage to change the things I can, and the wisdom to know the difference."

In that moment, we agreed we were together on a perfectly imperfect journey. We weren't striving for perfection; we were seeking serenity. When we are together, we are almost always hand in hand. It is one way we share our love, and it has also become a way we share our strength. As Jack's direct memory of me fades, he is still reaching for my hand whenever we are together.

Emotions are Contagious

Now that I practice massive acceptance of our journey and stay radically present in it, I have turned unhealthy fear into positive potential. I have no more unhealthy fear and no more F.E.A.R. I focus on what I can control. I work with the individuals who are the best resources for what is beyond my control and I let go of the rest. This gives me great peace and allows me to bring peace and positive energy with me when I am around my care receiver. During my research, I found multiple studies agreeing on the findings that emotions are contagious—for all of us! We all "catch" the emotions, positive and negative, of those around us[61]. As thinking and memories decline for individuals with types of dementia, they are more sensitive to, and mirror the emotions of, those around them[62]. I learned this the hard way during my dad's journey and wish I'd known it earlier. I would definitely have changed how I was with him in some of our experiences together, especially one in particular.

I was watching my dad one evening while Donna ran errands. One of his chores was walking the dog. My dad wanted to take the dog out. He started going out the back-screen door of their lanai onto the deep grass and down the sloped hill of their yard. I immediately focused on how unsafe this was for him and how bad it would be if he fell. I tried to prevent him from going that way. He was firm that this was the way he wanted to go. I grew increasingly concerned and told him how unsafe it was, especially since it was now dusk and hard to see. He grew increasingly firm and was now agitated. I reached for him and he pulled his arm from me. Now he was mad. He stormed down the hill with the dog who was, by now, also agitated and dancing around.

I was in a panic. I didn't realize how unsettling my tone of voice and my actions were to my dad. I was so upset by what happened that I wasn't calm and happy the rest of the evening and neither was my dad. Poor Donna! She came home to an upset husband and a scared daughter. I wish I'd known then what I know now. It was such a powerful lesson. It keeps me hyper-focused and intentional—radically present. I make sure I step into the experience of my care receiver to understand their perspective, and act from there.

Once I learned this lesson, it's the way I was with my dad every time we were together, and our future experiences were positive, even if the situation was challenging.

When I am with Jack, if I stay positive and calm, he usually does, too. If he is ever upset by something, I acknowledge it, and tell him I understand why he feels the way he does. I then focus even more intently on being calm and happy with him, finding things to smile and laugh about. I get right up close to his face, give him a big smile and say something kind and affirming to him.

Full disclosure: I have recently realized there is one thing that can take me away from staying 100% radically present with him. I have been keeping my cell phone with me, looking at it periodically, and sometimes responding to texts and emails. When I do this, I'm taking my attention away from him, and it disturbs my intention of staying focused on our experience together. I have now quit bringing my cell phone with me during my time with Jack unless it's for taking photos or videos together.

The Quilt of Our Lives

The quilt of our lives tells our story. I create mine through the clarity of my experiences. When my care receiver can no longer create theirs, we create it together. We share its beauty.

My best friend, Lynn, is an incredibly gifted quilter. Each of her quilts is an amazing work of art and are unique gifts of both beauty and story. I remember being with her as she carefully chose each piece of fabric for one of her creations. When I looked at the pieces, I couldn't tell what the quilt would look like. Once her quilt was assembled, piece by piece, and stitch by stitch, it was breathtaking, and I could see the story she was telling through it. I have a quilt she made me forty years ago. It is as beautiful today as it was when I first received it. I see it every day and there are still times I look at it and see something in a way I hadn't seen before.

Quilts, and the quilt-making process, are frequently used as metaphors for our lives and I understand why. Each piece of fabric in the quilt of our lives is one of our life experiences. Some of our experiences are intensely exciting and happy, perhaps represented by vibrant yellow silks. Some of our experiences are deeply sad, perhaps a deep purple tweed. Some are peaceful, like softly flowered flannel. Some are confusing and frustrating, like a rough beige burlap. Some of our experiences represent our strength and resilience, perhaps a rich red corduroy. Some of our experiences give us hope, perhaps a bright green crepe.

While my friend was creating each beautiful quilt, I would look at its front, see pieces here and there that weren't yet connected, places where pieces were missing, stitches not yet bringing the pieces together, and some of the frayed edges not yet protected by stitches. When I turned the quilt over, and looked at how the pieces were held together, I saw the power of the fabric as the quilt of our lives. Where I saw a rich velvet on the front side, on the back I saw the plain backing of the fabric that supported its beauty and the frayed edges of the fabric that reminded me many things that aren't beautiful go into creating great beauty. Where I saw the beautiful meandering stitches that traveled across groups of fabrics on the front, on the back I saw the threads' knots that represented starts and stops along the way. Where I saw the textured burlap on the front, I saw how very small the stitches were in order to hold the burlap closely to the other pieces and prevent its threads from unraveling, giving strength to its weakness. Where I saw unfinished edges with pieces missing around them, I saw lessons yet to be learned, experiences yet to happen. The quilt that was already there was ready to support what came next.

When my friend's quilt was finished, those pieces that didn't match, with their variety of colors, textures, shapes and sizes, all fit together beautifully. The frayed edges were all secured by stitches that protected them. Like the agreement my husband and I had about our journey being perfectly imperfect, the quilt that had *seemed* imperfect along the way was actually perfect the whole time. The experiences that create the fabric of the quilt of our lives and the stitches that bring and hold them together, create the unique and beautiful masterpiece of our life. I couldn't see it in the beginning; my friend could.

I am creating the quilt of my life based on how I choose to feel about each of my experiences. Through massive acceptance and radical presence, I choose my authentic expression for each experience. Living with my own definitions and not the labels of others means choosing how I represent each experience. I choose whether my challenges make me angry or strong. I choose whether I see beauty or ugliness in each moment, in each experience. I choose whether I am at peace or unrest in my experiences.

When I am practicing massive acceptance, radical presence, and self-care, I am able to choose each of the pieces of fabric in the quilt of my life.

I consciously choose the stitches I use to hold experiences together. Sometimes I use stitches I can see as I sew the pieces, I want these stitches as a clear reminder of what holds me together. Sometimes I use stitches I can't see yet I know they're there. Even though my experiences may seem to flow together smoothly, I know the placement of each knot. I know the exact location of each important rough spot that teaches me balance and gives me strength.

For me, the quilt as the metaphor for my life is more than a figure of speech. Thinking consciously of the quilt in terms of my life, and the life of my care receiver, helps me connect the importance of my choices with how I am creating my life and how I am serving as a steward for theirs.

When I'm in an experience, I make sure I'm accepting the experience for exactly what it is and I'm staying radically present in it. I say to myself, "What kind of fabric in the quilt of my life do I choose to represent this experience?" My journey isn't easy and I'm not asking for that, I'm creating it so it's authentic to who I am.

I'm creating my life quilt to represent the resilience I've learned with stitches that hold my experiences closely together, so I don't "fray at the edges." I'm creating my life quilt to represent the beauty I see in the moments so I smile when I look at it. I'm creating my life quilt to represent how I honestly feel in each experience so it represents me authentically and not someone else. I'm creating my life quilt to be strong so I can share it with others. I'm creating my life quilt to represent my life well lived.

As a metaphor for our lives, the quilt also represents the oneness of the journey of my care receiver and me. It includes us sharing the pieces of our quilt with each other, stitching them carefully into both our quilts. When my care receiver is no longer able to choose the perfect piece of fabric to represent their experience, I am. Being on the same journey, I now know what piece of fabric they would choose, I would choose the same one. I know where they would stitch it and what kind of stitches they would use. I would do the same. I knot their threads so that their quilt continues to become the quilt of their life, telling a beautiful story of their moments, their resilience, and their life well lived. Their quilt and mine continue in their creation so they can be shared with others and touch their lives in a positive way.

My goal for *Our Journey of Love: 5 Steps to Navigate Your Caregiving Journey* is that as you create the unique and beautiful quilt of your life, you are pleased with how it represents your life well lived. As you share it with others, it touches their lives with beauty and positivity.

The Paths of Our Journey

When we step into the perspective of each other's experiences,
we create our meaningful mutual experience—
with purpose and love.

For many years, I have thought of my journey in roles of care support and the journey my care receiver as our journey together. I didn't realize I was still looking from the perspective of my experiences, *and* from the perspective of my care receivers' experiences. It was as though in the beginning we were on separate paths that crossed every once in a while. As we experienced more together, our paths followed the same direction more frequently and became more and more deeply connected. We were physically together for many of the experiences of our journeys and our paths began to intertwine, and we were each still walking along our own path.

For their part of the journey, I walked along side my care receiver in their experiences. I focused on how I could help them, and how I could stay aware of what they needed. I made it my highest priority to keep them safe and help to create and support the environment that gave them their best opportunity to be happy.

For my part of the journey, my care receiver walked along side me as I focused on how I could stay healthy, so I had the capacity to be present for them and make sure they were provided the best support for their journey. I focused on massive acceptance and radical presence, so I was authentically participating in each of their experiences and mine.

We're on the Same Journey

I was talking with my treasured friend, Cynthia, about why I named my business *Our Journey of Love*. It's very simple; the care giver and care receiver come together on a journey where one of us accepts the role of support for the person who needs care. For me, this acceptance is one born out of a type of love.

I see the experiences of our roles—care support and care receiving—as being our journey together. I shared with Cynthia that, even with this as my perspective, I had recently begun to feel like something was missing and I wasn't sure what. Cynthia asked me the insightful question of what I meant by "our journey together."

Have you ever had an "ah ha" moment so powerful you had to pause to process it; a realization that changed your perspective forever? You suddenly had a new and clear vision, and you understood something in a different way. Once you began exploring your realization, the more obvious it seemed and the more energized you became.

I realized how many similarities exist in the care receiver and care giver experiences. We had a joint epiphany[63], realizing what it was I felt was missing.

We're not on two journeys, we're on one journey.

We are each engaging in our experiences from our unique perspectives. When we step into the perspective of each other's experiences, we create one meaningful mutual experience, with purpose.

Through practicing massive acceptance and radical presence, I step into my care receiver's experience and support them stepping into mine. We share it, we teach each other, and we help each other. Sometimes our intertwining is obvious, sometimes it's very subtle.

In Step 2, I mentioned one concrete way of stepping into a care receiver's experience: becoming part of a simulation exercise. Immersing myself in my care receiver's experiences with as many of my senses as possible, heightens my respect for them and helps me share with them so we participate together as fully as possible.

Instead of focusing on the experiences of the care giver and the experiences of the care receiver as separate, I now focus on the oneness of co-creating our journey. I now see our journey through the depth and breadth of our collective perspectives.

When we step into each other's experiences, we intentionally:

- Find purpose for our journey.
- Experience our journey through each other's hearts, minds, and feelings.
- Use empathy as our foundation and lens for our experiences.
- Ensure our actions are expressions of compassionate intent.
- Gain clarity about our feelings in each experience of our journey.

- Reciprocate care, trust, support, strength, and love.
- Expand our perspectives through the differences in how we relate to our experiences.
- Have unquenchable curiosity about how to improve our journey.
- Practice the massive acceptance and radical presence that creates the space for us to maximize our experiences.

If we begin our journey together this way, when my care receiver's capacity to practice intentionality diminishes, I know how to continue. Just like my dad taught me how to think like him so I could "talk" with him when he wasn't there, my care receiver teaches me how to experience our journey together as one.

What Does Oneness Look Like?

We are on the same journey when we are fully engaged in each other's experiences.

I studied mathematics for many years. One of the things I studied was Venn diagrams. These diagrams illustrate the relationships between things that share something in common[64]. I used to think about my journey with my care receiver like that. I was on my journey and my care receiver was on theirs. Our journey's intersected where we shared the common components created by our relationship with the diagnosis.

Seeing our journey as the same changes how I see the intersection of our lives. We are on the same path together; we are in the same experiences together. We participate in our experiences intentionally to participate through each other's perspective, so we know how to best support each other.

When one of us is not strong enough, the other person becomes our strength.

Now, I no longer see the caregiving/receiving journey as a Venn diagram. The image I see is each of us taking the steps of our journey side by side, strengthening each other, and when we cannot walk on our own, one of us carries the other. In the metaphor of the quilt, it's when we share the fabric in our life quilts. Our stitches become smaller and stronger, to keep our edges from fraying.

If you are a person of Christian faith, this is the message of the poem *Footprints in the Sand*[65],[66]. If you're not a person of faith, the message of the poem is that more than walking side by side with our care receiver, there are times when one of us "carries" the other, each in our own ways, through our journey together.

Footprints in the Sand
One night a man had a dream. He dreamed he was walking along the beach with the LORD.

Across the sky flashed scenes from his life. For each scene he noticed two sets of footprints in the sand: one belonging to him, and the other to the LORD.

When the last scene of his life flashed before him, he looked back at the footprints in the sand.
He noticed that many times along the path of his life there was only one set of footprints.

He also noticed that it happened at the very lowest and saddest times in his life.

This really bothered him and he questioned the LORD about it: "LORD, you said that once I decided to follow you, you'd walk with me all the way.

But I have noticed that during the most troublesome times in my life, there is only one set of footprints. I don't understand why when I needed you most you would leave me."

The LORD replied:

"My son, my precious child,
I love you and I would never leave you.
During your times of trial and suffering,
when you see only one set of footprints,
it was then that I carried you."

Our Journey and Perspective

Below is one example of the oneness of our journeys and one example of the oneness of our perspectives.

The Care Giver's Journey

One day, we wake up in our normal world. The next day, we want a Ph.D. in something that has shaken our world and changed its path dramatically. All kinds of thoughts are bouncing around in our minds like lottery draw machines[67]! We don't know what we don't know, we don't know to whom we should talk or what to do next. Questions are coming at us faster than we can even consider them. We want to be calm for our loved one, so they don't see our fear and because we know they have enough of their own.

Our emotions include fear, anger, sadness, frustration, confusion, uncertainty, overwhelm, helplessness. We know we want to do everything we can to make our experience the best it possibly can be for all of us. We want to help our loved one and we don't know where to start.

The Care Receiver's Journey

One day, we wake up in our normal world. The next day, we want a Ph.D. in something that has shaken our world and changed its path dramatically. All kinds of thoughts are bouncing around in our minds like lottery draw machines (67)! We don't know what we don't know, we don't know to whom we should talk or what to do next. Questions are coming at us faster than we can even consider them. We want to be calm for our loved one, so they don't see our fear and because we know they have enough of their own.

Our emotions include fear, anger, sadness, frustration, confusion, uncertainty, overwhelm, helplessness. We know we want to do everything we can to make our experience the best it possibly can be for all of us. We want to help our loved one and we don't know where to start.

The Care Giver's Perspective

My life as I knew it has suddenly changed. I don't yet know the impact. Everything seems different today. I don't know how to feel about this and I think I may be afraid to find out.

The Care Receiver's Perspective

My life as I knew it has suddenly changed. I don't yet know the impact. Everything seems different today. I don't know how to feel about this and I think I may be afraid to find out.

When We're Not Strong Enough

I have listened to, and been touched by, many inspirational speeches throughout my life. Two of them have been very insightful for me as I embrace them through the lens of being on our care journey together. When I heard these speeches originally, I was listening from the perspective of a care giver: what I could do *for* my care receiver so they could have their best journey, their best life. My perspective now includes our gaining clarity on this together and supporting each other.

The first speech was in 1993, when basketball player, coach, and broadcaster, Jim Valvano received the inaugural Arthur Ashe Courage and Humanitarian award[68] at the ESPY's show (Excellence in Sports Performance Yearly Awards). In his speech, Valvano talked about how cancer had touched his life. He exclaimed with much emotion that it couldn't touch his heart, mind, or soul. He shared how the disease had given him a new and clear purpose to his life that wasn't just for his life, it was for generations to come.

His purpose was to find cures and breakthroughs for cancer so others can survive and prosper. He did that by starting a foundation in his name for cancer research. His purpose informed how he lived each day. The motto of his foundation is, "Don't give up, don't ever give up." It has already awarded over $200 million in cancer research grants nationwide, while also receiving a 94.69 out of 100 rating by Charity Navigator, the nation's largest and most-utilized evaluator of charities.[69]

In his closing, Jim Valvano restated his perspective and his purpose:

Cancer can take away all my physical abilities. It cannot touch my mind, it cannot touch my heart and it cannot touch my soul. And those three things are going to carry on forever.

When my care receiver and I have each have clarity on our purpose, our experiences are not just "ours" and "theirs." As much as they can, our experiences become part of each other's hearts, minds, and souls. We consider each other's perspectives with our feelings, thoughts, emotions, and actions.

As the journey of my care receiver progresses, they may no longer have access to their purpose directly. I continue to help them live their life with their purpose, and I continue to live mine inclusive of theirs. This was brought home to me through another speech given in the sports community. It was to someone receiving the Jim Valvano Perseverance award.

At the 2014 ESPY's, ESPN anchor, Stuart Scott, received their annual Jimmy V. Perseverance Award. It recognizes "a deserving member of the sporting world who has overcome great obstacles through perseverance and determination[70]." The award was named in honor of Jim Valvano, who passed away less than two months after he gave his speech at the 1993 ESPY's.

Throughout the eight years of Stuart Scott's journey with cancer, he lived his life as a model of perseverance and created opportunities for us to be inspired in our own journeys. During Stuart Scott's speech, I listened as he spoke honestly and candidly about his journey. I watched the video montage showing his journey of memories created and messages shared by his friends and daughters. I found myself stepping into his emotions and the emotions of their experience. The cameras filming the ESPY's panned the crowd periodically throughout Scott's speech and I cried with them. I stepped into how he was feeling, and how those around him were feeling, as he went through treatment after treatment.

I saw what I was meant to see in his experience; how the perspective of his disease had inspired him—and those around him— to find a new purpose in their lives.

Without realizing its full impact, I felt like, as a care giver, I was on the same journey with my care receiver. I felt what Stuart felt. I felt what the other care givers felt. I heard how the love and strength of those who surrounded him strengthened and sustained him. I heard and felt how important their support was for him. I felt the grief his daughters expressed.

One excerpt of Mr. Scott's speech touched me deeply as a care giver. Looking back, it was the first time I connected the power of our journey with the potential of its purpose in our lives. It strengthened my commitment to making sure I keep my grace of space, so I stay present and strong throughout our entire journey.

Scott said:

When you die, that does not mean that you lose to cancer. You beat cancer by how you lived, why you lived and in the manner in which you lived. So live. Live. Fight like hell. And when you get too tired to fight, then lay down and rest and let somebody else fight for you[71].

My takeaways from his message are that during my care receiver's journey and when my care receiver dies, he or she did not lose to their disease. They lived their life with purpose. The disease was part of their life and it had purpose in their life, and it was not all their life was. While I am giving care in roles of support, I am living my life with purpose. The experiences of our journey together are part of my life and they have purpose in my life, and they are not all my life is. We help each other make the most of our experiences and live our best lives through our journey together.

Our journey is bigger than each of us. When we are both strong enough, we fight together as hard as we can. When one of us becomes too tired to fight, we know we can lay down and rest, and the other will continue the fight for both of us.

I now see, even more clearly, the importance of inviting others into our journey. When they want to help, we let them bring their strength. Sometimes they become our strength.

A diagnosis can ignite the purpose in each of us. I make sure I am clear about my purpose for our journey together and help my care receiver live theirs.

Making the Experience Bigger Than Me

I am created to thrive in my life and feel great about myself, so I make my most positive impact in our world. When I make experiences bigger than I am, I am who I am created to be.

My vision with *Our Journey of Love: 5 Steps to Navigate Your Caregiving Journey*, is to help everyone in roles of care support positively navigate their journey, the journey of their care receiver, and the journeys of those who support them.

One of the areas of struggle during my roles of care support is the availability of respite care to support those in caregiving roles – both professionals and those of us who are not professionally trained.

Just as I feel strongly about writing this book as one way to pay my gratitude forward for those who help me, I know it is also meant to be a resource to help create opportunities for respite care.

At the time I am writing this book, I haven't finalized what this looks like. I do know I am donating 50% of the proceeds from everything I do with *Our Journey of Love,* to the creation and support of respite care offerings.

Rather than creating my own respite care facilities, I will find places around the world who will benefit in the great work they are already doing. These places provide the important resources to support the caregivers' efforts, so care receivers thrive, feel great about themselves and make a positive impact in our world.

Thank you for being part of making our world a better place through your support.

The Caregiver's Affirmation

An affirmation is a statement of something that is true, to publicly show your support for an opinion or idea[72]. When writing *Our Journey of Love: 5 Steps to Navigate Your Caregiving Journey*, I wrote an affirmation at the beginning of each chapter. It states what has become truth for me during each step of my journeys in roles of care support.

A friend of mine asked me to read each of my affirmations out loud to her. As I did, we both realized that collectively they represent a beautiful picture of what the caregiving journey can be.

I now share with you all of the affirmations together and invite you to consider them for yourselves.

The Caregiver's Affirmation

I'm always doing my very best with where I am at. I find coping mechanisms to support me staying emotionally balanced on my journey.

This is my journey. Beliefs are my compass. Intention is my guide. Self-care is my fuel. I only get lost if I travel someone else's journey.

I choose to care from a place of love.

I will never be alone. Help and care are all around me. I receive so I can give.

Massive acceptance and radical presence give me the gift of living each moment from its greatest potential.

The quilt of our lives tells our story. I create mine through the clarity of my experiences. When my care receiver can no longer create theirs, we create it together. We share its beauty.

When we step into the perspective of each other's experiences, we create our meaningful mutual experience—with purpose and love.

I am created to thrive in my life and feel great about myself, so I make my most positive impact in our world. When I make experiences bigger than I am, I am who I am created to be.

Simulation Exercises

Virtual dementia experience: https://www.awalkthrough.org

Vision simulator:
https://www.perkinselearning.org/scout/blog/simulation-vision-conditions

Exercises that simulate challenges of a variety of disabilities:
https://www.dvusd.org/cms/lib/AZ01901092/Centricity/Domain/1318/Disability%20Awareness%20Packet%202.pdf

Simulations of a variety of traumatic events including stroke:
https://www.sitelms.org/catalog/search//?keywords=simulation&publish_status%5B%5D=Active

Citations

[1] https://www.psychiatry.org/psychiatrists/practice/dsm/educational-resources/dsm-5-fact-sheets

[2] https://www.mdedge.com/neurology/article/81892/alzheimers-cognition/dementia-officially-replaced-major-neurocognitive

[3] https://web.library.yale.edu/cataloging/music/historyof78rpms

[4] https://medical-dictionary.thefreedictionary.com/coping+mechanism

[5] https://www.merriam-webster.com/dictionary/stress

[6] https://www.inc.com/lolly-daskal/how-to-be-more-resilient-when-things-get-tough.html

[7] http://leadershipintelligence.com/emerging-leaders/resiliency-a-trait-you-develop-not-one-youre-born-with/

[8] https://www.merriam-webster.com/dictionary/resilience

[9] https://writingexplained.org/resilience-vs-resiliency-difference

[10] https://dictionary.cambridge.org/us/dictionary/english/resilience

[11] http://northpointministries.org

[12] https://horsley.yale.edu/resilience

[13] https://definitions.uslegal.com/c/caregiver/

[14] https://www.merriam-webster.com/dictionary/care

[15] https://www.merriam-webster.com/dictionary/giver

[16] https://www.merriam-webster.com/dictionary/guide

[17] https://www.merriam-webster.com/dictionary/partner

[18] https://www.merriam-webster.com/dictionary/supports

[19] https://www.lexico.com/en/definition/self

[20] https://www.huffingtonpost.com/margaret-moodian/lessons-of-compassion-fro_b_7868940.html

[21] https://www.merriam-webster.com/dictionary/worry

[22] https://www.goodreads.com/quotes/201777-i-ve-had-a-lot-of-worries-in-my-life-most

[23] https://www.care.com/c/stories/14923/40-inspirational-caregiver-quotes/

[24] https://www.merriam-webster.com/dictionary/guilt

[25] https://www.merriam-webster.com/dictionary/sorry

[26] http://webhome.auburn.edu/~mitrege/ENGL2210/USNWR-mind.html

[27] https://www.centeronaddiction.org/what-addiction/addiction-disease

28 https://www.ncbi.nlm.nih.gov/pmc/articles/PMC5645519/
29 http://www.compassionfatigue.org
30 https://www.goodtherapy.org/blog/134-activities-to-add-to-your-self-care-plan/
31 https://www.paulpearsall.com/info/about.html
32 https://www.historydisclosure.com/transplant-recipients-pick-up-the-memories-of-their-donors/
33 https://www.slideshare.net/manu123a/the-hearts-code
34 https://www.ncbi.nlm.nih.gov/pmc/articles/PMC4104432/
35 https://www.enneagraminstitute.com
36 https://www.mayoclinic.org/diseases-conditions/alzheimers-disease/expert-answers/music-and-alzheimers/faq-20058173
37 http://anxietytreatmentexperts.com/equine-assisted-therapy/
38 http://lindabucher.com/wp-content/uploads/2012/04/What-Happy-People-Know-Book-Discussion.pdf
39 https://www.alzheimers.net/stages-of-alzheimers-disease/
40 https://www.alz.org/alzheimers-dementia/stages
41 https://newsroom.fb.com/company-info/
42 https://www.wonderopolis.org/wonder/do-elephants-ever-forget
43 https://www.constitution.org/col/blind_men.htm
44 https://blog.nationalgeographic.org/2017/06/17/using-positive-feedback-for-training-elephants-in-thailand/
45
https://www.elephant.se/elephant_training_history.php?open=Elephant%2
0training
46
https://www.barrypopik.com/index.php/new_york_city/entry/how_do_you
_eat_an_elephant
47 https://knowyourphrase.com/elephant-in-the-room
48 https://www.collectivenounslist.com/elephants
49 https://thesystemsthinker.com/human-dynamics-for-the-21st-century/
50 https://www.merriam-webster.com/dictionary/hope
51 https://www.pursuit-of-happiness.org/history-of-happiness/viktor-frankl/
52 https://www.stlyrics.com/lyrics/carousel/youllneverwalkalone.htm
53 https://dictionary.cambridge.org/us/dictionary/english/massive

54 https://medium.com/oxford-university/the-amazing-phenomenon-of-muscle-memory-fb1cc4c4726
55 https://teepasnow.com
56 https://teepasnow.com/wp-content/uploads/2019/01/HO-Improving-

Connection-During-Times-of-Distress-San-Jose.pdf

[57] https://www.goodreads.com/quotes/51356-everything-can-be-taken-from-a-man-but-one-thing

[58] http://www.compassionfatigue.org/pages/caregiverexchange.pdf

[59] http://www.compassionfatigue.org

[60] https://www.smithsonianmag.com/science-nature/what-happens-brain-feel-fear-180966992/

[61] https://www.canr.msu.edu/news/emotions_are_contagious_learn_what_science_and_research_has_to_say_about_it

[62] https://www.webmd.com/alzheimers/news/20130528/alzheimers-patients-mimic-emotions-of-those-around-them-study#1

[63] https://www.merriam-webster.com/dictionary/epiphany

[64] https://whatis.techtarget.com/definition/Venn-diagram

[65] https://en.wikipedia.org/wiki/Footprints_(poem)

[66] https://www.scrapbook.com/poems/doc/38987.html

[67] https://www.thelotter.com/lottery-machines/

[68] https://www.v.org/about/remembering-jim/espy-awards-speech/

[69] https://www.charitynavigator.org/index.cfm?bay=search.summary&orgid=5907

[70] https://www.huffpost.com/entry/stuart-scott-espys-jimmy-v-perseverance-award_n_5594242

[71] https://www.youtube.com/watch?v=4TdF07xO-eo

[72] https://dictionary.cambridge.org/us/dictionary/english/affirm

Made in the USA
Columbia, SC
16 December 2019